④ TYPES

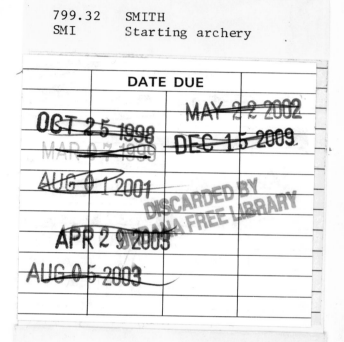

DATE DUE		
OCT 25 1998	MAY 2 2 2002	
MAR 0 7 1999	DEC 1 5 2009	
AUG 0 1 2001		
APR 2 9 2003		
AUG 0 5 2003		

DISCARDED BY
URBANA FREE LIBRARY

Starting Archery

Starting Archery

Mike Smith

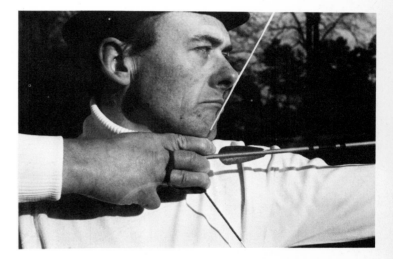

ARCO PUBLISHING COMPANY, INC.
New York

Acknowledgements
The author wishes to express his sincere appreciation to the following people for their valuable help in the production of this book: Peter Saunders of Aylesbury Toxophily Crafts Ltd.; Johnson & Starley Ltd., in particular Mrs K. Forskitt; Aviette Kits for the use of their grounds; and the following archers and coaches who were generous with their help in various ways: John Miller, Guy Ely, Don Stamp, Rodger Tapp and Ellis Shepherd who originally proposed that he should write the book.
The jacket photographs are by Colorsport.
  Special thanks go to Peter Crawley and John Wright who took most of the photographs illustrating this book. Finally, the author thanks his wife Ann who typed the manuscript, and showed infinite patience and understanding, and to whom this book is dedicated.

Published by Arco Publishing Company, Inc.

219 Park Avenue South, New York, N.Y. 10003

Copyright © 1978 by Mike Smith

Printed in Great Britain

Published in Great Britain by Ward Lock Limited, a member of the Pentos Group

Library of Congress Cataloging in Publishing Data

Smith, Mike.
Archery.

1. Archery. I. Title.
GV1185.S59   1978   799.3'2   78-3829
ISBN 0 668 04633 3

Contents

Foreword

This book, intended as a guide to those starting archery, will be of great value. In an easy-to read style, it goes into full details of the sport, from individual items of tackle and basic technique, to self analysis and the correction of shooting faults leading to improvement in shooting style.

The beginner at the sport, as well as the novice archer without the benefit of qualified instruction or coaching, will find the contents of great assistance in acquiring a good shooting technique.

Ellis Shepherd
National Coaching Organiser
Grand National Archery Society

1 Starting archery

The modern sport of archery, or shooting with a bow, is an adaptation of man's traditional use for bow and arrows; that is to defend and feed his family. The bow is probably man's first invention of a device in which energy can be accumulated slowly, stored temporarily and released suddenly with great speed and accuracy.

The invention dates back as many as 30 000 years and up until the sixteenth century, the bow was man's constant companion in almost every part of the world. In English history, the longbow will always hold a special place for the victories it won at Crécy, Agincourt and Poitiers. Genghis Khan's horsemen shot the short composite bow from the backs of their galloping horses, during the Mongol conquests. More recently, the American Indians used the bow as a means of subsistence, bringing down heavy buffalo with a short flat bow, and also as a means of defence against the white settlers.

After its replacement by firearms as weapons of war, the bow became a favourite weapon of sport. Hunting with bow and arrow is still practised, particularly in the United States and Canada, where a short bow-hunting season precedes the firearms season. However, today, Target and Field archery are the most popular forms and the ones that are usually taken up by beginners. This book will deal with the basic principles of starting these forms of archery.

Modern archery is organised in Great Britain by the Grand National Archery Society (GNAS) which in recent years has incorporated Field Archery. In the United States of America the National Archery Association of the United States (NAA) is the official governing body. These and other national associations listed in the appendix are affiliated to the Federation Internationale de Tir à l'Arc (FITA) which is the world governing body recognized by the International Olympic Committee. All the officially recognized organizations of the member nations of FITA send competitors to the World Championships, and when appropriate, to the Olympic Games.

A clear avenue exists therefore for a dedicated person to begin this fascinating sport and continue to the top, if that is his wish. Most will prefer to keep archery as a healthy and entertaining hobby; whatever the ambitions of the beginner, all sorts of possibilities are offered within the sport. Besides conventional archery there are several other types of archery which give some variety.

Target archery

Target archery is the most popular in Great Britain, at least numerically, and in most parts of the country a club can be found within a reasonable distance. Target archery originated from martial sources. Battles in olden times tended to be set pieces with the opposing forces drawn up in more or less regular patterns. The usual practice of the British archers in these battles was to bombard the enemy lines, when they advanced. Eventually they would be shooting directly at them; that is to say, aiming their arrows rather than bombarding and the range would gradually reduce as the opposing sides closed. Thus in target competition rounds the longest distances are shot first and then reduced as the tournament proceeds.

Some significance may be attached to the fact that none of the English traditional rounds had a distance shorter than 40 yards! Perhaps at that distance there was just enough time to abandon the bow and take up close quarter weapons.

This form of archery is shot over open flat ground at targets of 4 feet (122 cm) diameter and a round would comprise a set number of arrows shot at the various distances. The British or NAA rounds use the same large targets at all distances but in the International or FITA rounds the target size is reduced at the shorter distances of 50 metres and 30 metres to one of 80 cm diameter.

The GNAS and NAA target face is divided into five colour zones which are gold in the centre, then red, blue, black and white which score 9,7,5,3, and 1 respectively. The FITA target faces of 122 cm or 80 cm are coloured and divided similarly, except that each colour zone is divided to give an inner gold and two equal widths of each colour. This is scored 10 at the centre reducing to 1 on the outer white.

The most testing of the GNAS and NAA rounds are the

Championship Rounds, which for men is the York round and for women the Hereford round. These both require 144 arrows to be shot, usually over a complete day's shooting and for men are distributed as follows; six dozen arrows at 100 yards, four dozen at 80 yards, and two dozen at 60 yards. The women shoot six dozen at 80 yards, four dozen at 60 yards and two dozen at 50 yards. The FITA rounds are metric and three dozen arrows are shot at each of the distances which are 90, 70, 50 and 30 metres for men and 70, 60, 50 and 30 metres for women. There are in fact seventeen different rounds from which to choose and some of the shorter rounds, both in distance and number of arrows shot, make an ideal start for the new archer.

Juniors are catered for by rounds designed to suit the ages of 18 years, 16 years, 14 years, 13 years and 12 years. These rounds are known as Bristol Rounds and are carefully designed to be an appropriate challenge to suit the age of the archer. The ages are the top limit for a given section but there is no objection to a younger child shooting.

1. Junior archers shooting in a match.

Indoor archery

Indoor shooting is a valuable part of the archery scene in the Northern States of America and throughout Canada where the hard winters prevent regular outdoor activities. In a number of centres in America there are indoor shooting ranges which operate rather like bowling alleys where archers can shoot from fixed positions and a mechanized system brings the targets to the archer for recovery and scoring of arrows. Even without access to these facilities it is valuable in the winter to hire suitable halls and continue shooting in order to keep club members together and keep up regular practice. Most countries have now recognized the value of indoor shooting and have, through their national organizations, established approved rounds and hold championship events.

Field archery

2. Field archers combat natural hazards.

This form of archery developed out of the sport of hunting with bow and arrow. The skill of woodcraft, of reading tracks and stalking the quarry are all lost in Field archery since the targets are fixed and will not disappear at the first scent of man or the first twang of a bow string. Nevertheless the sport is very testing of shooting skills.

The course is usually laid out in rough country, wooded areas, or scrubland and should be sharply undulating terrain. This provides a wide number of natural hazards upon which a field course can be constructed. Generally, a Field course is rather like a Golf course in that it is progressive. Archers shoot on one target, go and score up and collect arrows, and move on to the next target. Layout of the course will to some extent be dependent on the terrain and space available, but a standard round would comprise twenty-eight targets. This can be arranged in one set of fourteen targets, known as a 'unit', shot over twice.

One great advantage of Field archery is the wide variety the sport can take. The targets vary in size from 6 inches (15 cm) diameter up to 24 inches (60 cm) in diameter and these are shot at from ranges as short as 5 yards up to 80 yards and when shooting FITA rounds the distances are between 5 metres and 60 metres. Needless to say, the smaller targets are used on the shorter distances. The distances being shot are not always indicated, so the field archer has not only to contend with the lie of the land and obstructions that might appear to make the shot more of a problem, but must also assess accurately the distance to the target. This is not at all easy as the shot may have to be taken uphill, downhill, over water or perhaps across a valley. This all conspires to make the shot more difficult and fully tests the field archer's ability.

There are two classes of archers in Field archery: the 'Bare Bow' class which comprises archers who do not use sights on their bows and are not allowed any attachments or marks that could be construed as an aid to aiming; and the 'Free Style' archer, who is allowed the use of a sight. This section of Field archery has considerable appeal to target archers, who can enjoy an occasional Field Shoot without having to make a radical change of technique. Naturally, the two classes do not compete, since archers using sights could be held to have the advantage.

As a further variety, there are specialist rounds to be enjoyed. The Hunter's Round uses target faces coloured in black, with only a white aiming mark which can be seen from the shooting position. This adds to the difficulty of assessing the distances to be shot over. The Big Game Round is shot on target faces depicting various animals and birds. The target is divided into zones described as killing or

3. Barebow archers shooting the slopes.

wounding zones, with appropriate scoring values. The special interest lies in the fact that three arrows are allowed to be shot at each target, the first from the longest of three distances identified (but not necessarily stated) by posts, the second a bit closer, and the third from the shortest distance. Only one arrow is scored and as soon as the target is hit no more may be shot. The value of the longest shot is higher than the second shot or shortest shot progressively when scoring so the arrows are marked to indicate the order in which they are shot.

The fact that Field archery is mobile, in moving from one target to another, has a wide variety of targets and distances over which to shoot, and is over rough but natural open country, all combine to give this form of archery a very considerable appeal.

Bow hunting

Bow hunting is the original source of Field archery. However, hunting is still carried out in the United States and Canada and enjoys a very large following, especially in the United States.

16

Various regulations exist covering the weight of bow required as a minimum before licences can be issued and normally there are stringent restrictions on the game that may be taken, for conservation reasons. Small animals regarded as vermin, or creatures classified as such may not be covered by such regulations. Small animals and birds are usually hunted with arrows called blunts which kill by impact, which are special arrows with large diameter flat heads rather than sharp points.

Animals of any size, such as deer and larger, are usually taken using broadhead arrows which have spear-like heads sharpened for maximum penetration. For safety reasons, some game, such as moose and bear, should not be hunted by the bow hunter alone, but backed up by a heavy rifle in the hands of an expert.

In Great Britain, the occasions for bow hunting are very limited, and the GNAS does not support it.

Bow fishing

Fishing with the bow is very popular in some countries. A special arrow with a barbed head is used. It is attached to a line which is carried on a drum reel on the bow. Some very large fish have been taken with the bow and it demands great skill on the part of the archer to snap off the shot, allowing for refraction, to hit the fish and plant the barb. Spear fishing is illegal in Great Britain.

Clout shooting

The word clout is an old English word for a patch or piece of cloth, which would be used to mark the target, probably arranged as a flag or simply dropped to the ground. It is still practised in some clubs, particularly target archery clubs, as it has similarly military origins. In this form of shooting, the object is to bombard the 'enemy', now, happily replaced by a target.

The target area is 24 feet in diameter, marked out on the ground, and the centre is indicated by a white flag on a post near the ground. Shooting is carried out at a range of 180 yards for men and 140 yards for women, both distances being much greater than the direct shooting of the bow can reach. Thus, the arrows have to be lobbed at a relatively high angle so that they drop into the target.

Under FITA rules the target is 15 metres in diameter and is shot at ranges of 165 metres for men and 125 metres for women.

It is tremendous fun and much pleasure is gained by all who participate in it. In some clubs, a clout shoot is used to 'open' and 'close' the outdoor season. An unusual tradition that used to be carried out on more formal occasions was for an observer, dressed in frock coat and top hat, to stand some distance away from, and aside of, the 'clout' and if a direct hit was made on the clout he was expected to fall flat on his back! For other hits on the target area, he would simply wave his top hat: a curious custom, not recommended today.

Flight shooting

Flight shooting is similar to Clout in that long distances are involved, but in this case no attempt is being made to hit a target. The whole object is to see how far an arrow can be shot. Standard equipment can be used, but for serious flight shooting, a special bow design is required. This style of archery has its own special fascination and enjoys a limited, if enthusiastic, following.

Popinjay

Popinjay is another rather specialized form of archery, very popular in Holland and Belgium, in which the object is to shoot vertically upwards to dislodge 'birds' (made from cork and decorative feathers) from their perches some 85 to 90 feet (approx. 26 to 27 m) from the ground. Special arrows with large diameter blunt heads, rather than points, are used. A covered safety zone is provided for the archer to duck into as an essential precaution against the descending arrow.

Archery golf

When an archer has a golfer as a friend, it can sometimes be arranged for them to play a round together, each using the appropriate tackle. This is Archery Golf. An ordinary bow is used and normally three arrows, one a light arrow for 'driving', an ordinary arrow for the 'approach' shots and a special arrow with a spiked head for 'putting'. The 'hole' is provided by a white disc some 4 inches (10 cm) in diameter, placed near the hole on the green.

Archery for the disabled

Most countries, Great Britain and the United States included, changed their shooting regulations to permit the disabled archer to participate in archery events. In the case of a wheelchair archer the chair may stay on the shooting line once it has been positioned and need not move until a change of distance is made. Archers with disablement of the hands may employ devices to retain the bow in the bow hand, or if the disablement prevents normal loosing of the bow string, they may have a mechanical device to do so. This is at the discretion of the officials in charge of the shoot, since some devices could give an unreasonable advantage. However, archers and officials encourage the disabled to participate on equal terms with other competitors.

The disabled person who wishes to take up archery should do so only under the guidance of qualified help in order to be sure of being trained correctly and with proper regard to the nature of the disablement. Special methods and techniques have been developed and disabled archery is now worldwide.

The technique of archery

The basic purpose of any shooting technique is to enable the archer to shoot a number of arrows with maximum accuracy. Any method of shooting which would enable an archer to achieve this could be described as a good shooting technique. Before coaching systems existed, a novice would observe the shooting methods used by the top shots of the time, and seek to copy them. However, little was understood of how things worked, and often the top shot could not fully explain the reason for the success of the technique employed.

In general, it would be reasonable to consider a good shooting technique to possess the following qualities:

1 Can be performed whilst in a comfortable position.

2 A sequence of movements following a logical progression which is easy to remember.

3 Each movement can be fully explained and practised (in isolation from the others if need be).

4 Should encourage the correct use of muscles without inducing strain.

A system of shooting which meets these basic requirements would give a beginner a very firm base upon which to start. The objective is to produce a consistent result by the archer performing the technique in a consistent manner. This demands considerable concentration during the early stages and care taken in practice during these times will pay handsome dividends. The process of learning physical activities of any sort is the same for the body as for the mind. The activity has to be carried out using the full power of the mind to concentrate on what is being done, to ensure that it is being done correctly. The body feels, and records in the brain, the physical sensations of the activity being carried out.

Continuation of practice, or accurate repetition, allows the body to repeat the recording of the sensations associated with the activity and the brain begins to recognize a pattern. As stronger and stronger signals are sent to the various muscle groups involved it becomes a 'learned response' or 'conditioned reflex', and the body knows when the activity is being correctly duplicated because it *feels right*.

This sense of feel is an important part of an archer's technique. Once the conditioned reflexes are established the concentration of the concious thinking part of the brain can be redirected to those elements of the technique which will demand its attention however much experience an archer may have. A good example of this is sighting on the target.

Good shooting calls for a considerable degree of self discipline:

Self discipline applied to the initial learning process – to seek the best possible performance of each element of the technique on every occasion it is practised.

Self discipline applied to the aiming at the target to be satisfied only with a well-aimed shot. It is a pity to waste a good preparation by a badly aimed shot at the end of it all.

Self discipline in being prepared to break off the preparation sequence if the sense of feel indicates that all is not well. To be prepared to start all over again with a determined will to get it right.

Thus applied, self discipline will make the archer the master of the equipment and the master of the self and create that harmony of the mind and body with the equipment that will make the good shot possible. That is what archery is!

2 Equipment you may need

This book is primarily intended to help those who will take up either Target or Field archery. This will be largely influenced by the archery clubs which exist in the area and the facilities they have to offer.

Joining a club and learning to shoot there, is much better than trying to struggle along on your own. In addition, many clubs have a certain amount of equipment which may be borrowed, to give you an initial opportunity to try out the sport.

Not all clubs will have a recognized or qualified instructor or coach, but the more experienced members will be able to give some general ideas on the equipment you will need at the start.

Bow

Choosing the bow is the first step and the ideal type with which to learn to shoot is the fibre-glass self bow (that is, one piece of material) which can be supplied either flat or with reflexed tips, the latter being a little more expensive but because of the design of the bow will give better cast or throwing power than the flat one. There are various models produced by different manufacturers throughout the world.

The bow should have a rubber moulded or plastic handle and some models are shaped to make them suitable for left or right hand use. They are normally supplied complete with the bow string but will need a nocking point added to the centre section of the string to indicate where the arrow is to be fitted to the bow string each time.

Nocking point
There are various ways of indicating the nocking point. If the string diameter where the arrow goes is a good fit for the nock of the arrow, a simple method is to mark the string centre-serving in a contrasting colour, with a felt tip marker pen. When this is not practical because of the colour of the centre-serving, a thin strip of self-adhesive tape can be

Beginner's fibreglass bows.

Top At equal draw weight and draw length this design of bow will give a longer range than a flat bow.

Below This design of bow is rather easier to string than the other type.

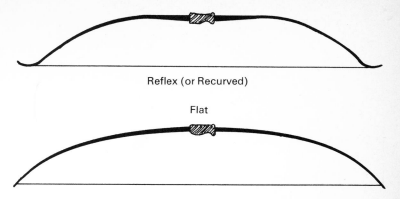

Reflex (or Recurved)

Flat

employed. Another method is to fit nock locaters onto the string with a special crimping tool, but this may mean an extra item of expenditure which is not essential at this time, if the club does not have one.

A simple test of the fit of the nock of the arrow on the bow string is to place the arrow on the string and see if it hangs on when the arrow is suspended vertically. It should require a light flick of the bow string to dislodge it (the exception being the keyhole clip-on nocks which will stay in place). If the arrow will not stay on, then the bow string will need to be thickened locally which can be done by winding on a few turns of 'dental floss' which can be obtained at any drug store or chemist. This would then act as the nocking point.

Sight
For target archery a simple sight will be required and this can be provided very easily by fixing a strip of draught-excluder foam to the back of the bow, running from the top of the handle and about six inches up the bow limb. The aiming device itself is a plastic headed dressmakers pin in a suitable colour, say black, which can be inserted into the foam and used for aiming. This should be tucked away in the top of the foam strip with the point well buried for the time being. The Field archer will not be using a sight so none of the above applies.

Choosing your bow
Under ideal conditions, when learning to shoot, a very light bow should be employed. The expression 'light bow' means that the draw weight, or the force required, is well

below the eventual capacity of the archer. This has the advantage that the new archer is not fighting the weight of the bow, as well as trying to learn good technique.

When a new archer has access to a club, there may be a light bow available, or one could be purchased with reasonable prospects of selling it later to another beginner joining the club. A suitable light bow would be 30 pounds at 28 inches, which means that the force applied to the bow string to bring it 28 inches away from the back of the bow would be 30 pounds. This would suit all sizes of archer since if the bow is not drawn 28 inches but only, say, 24 inches, the force required would be correspondingly less so the bow would be very versatile and suit anyone.

Arrows

These should be of the type made from aluminium tube and of a length which will be safe to use. A simple and effective way of checking this is to place the nock end (where the feathers are) against the chest, in line with the shoulders, with the shaft extending forward between the

4. Checking arrow length.

palms of the outstretched hands (see figure on page 24).

For Target archers there must be *at least* one inch projecting beyond the tips of the fingers, and for Field archers at least three inches projection. This allows for the occasional variation of draw length in the early stages of learning to shoot. A more accurate method of measuring draw length, for when you buy your own, will be described later on in the chapter.

It may be that you cannot borrow arrows and will have to buy some straight away, in which case the later notes in this chapter will apply *except* that the length must be checked as mentioned above. It may be possible to cut the length of the arrows down later or, perhaps, pass them on to another beginner, or trade them in.

Some parts of the arrow need to be identified and explained:

Shaft: simply refers to the tube from which the arrow is made.

Pile: the correct name for the point of the arrow which is shaped to penetrate the target.

Nock: the end of the arrow opposite the pile, with a groove arranged to fit onto the nocking point of the bow string.

Fletchings: the feathers or vanes fitted to the shaft to assist in stabilizing the arrow in flight. One of these is arranged at a right angle to the slot in the nock and may be a different colour to the other two. This is called the cock feather.

Crestings: the coloured bands around the arrows, just under the fletchings which assist in identifying your arrows in the target when you are shooting in company of others.

The remaining items of shooting equipment are a finger tab, a bracer and some form of quiver in which to place the arrows when shooting. The last two could be borrowed from the club, but the finger tab needs to be a correct fit and will have to be purchased and cut to a suitable shape to suit your hand. This is fully described later in the chapter see page 33.

After you have been shooting long enough to decide you enjoy the sport and are beginning to settle down into a reasonable technique, the natural step is to wish to purchase your own equipment.

Buying equipment and measuring-up

The Bow

A moderately priced composite bow, that is one made from laminations of wood and fibre-glass, is the best type to buy since its better performance will be needed in shooting over the longest ranges.

It is worth considering 'trade-in' bows a dealer may have in stock. These are usually the more advanced composite bows which you will want eventually and these trade-ins can often be an excellent bargain. Reputable dealers would not offer a defective bow, but few would object to your examining them before purchase.

There are a number of checks that should be carried out to ensure the bow is in good condition and these are shown in the diagram.

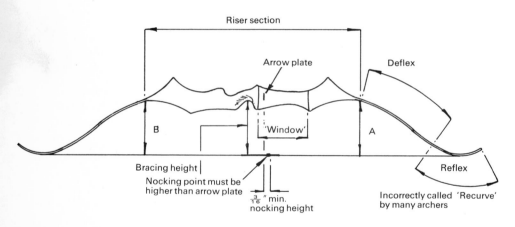

Checking for twist
Roll an arrow under the string on the 'high point' of the reflex on both limbs of the bow and sight along the bow string —the arrows should be in line—not 'crossed' as in the illustration above.

Draw weight

The draw weight of a bow will depend on the archer using it and the relationship which exists between the draw length and the desirable maximum weight of bow to be drawn.

For men this is draw length × 1.5 = weight of bow
For example: 26 in draw length × 1.5 = 39 lb draw weight
For women this is draw length × 1.1 = weight of bow
For example: 24 in draw length × 1.1 = 26.4 lb draw weight

so we would say 26 lbs.

26

These relationships apply to people of average build and strength, and variations from 'average' should be taken into account. For example, a lightly built person should use a bow of a couple of pounds less draw weight than the formula given, but a powerfully built person might use a pound or so more, but don't go up more than that. The formula is intended to avoid an archer being 'overbowed' which means trying to cope with a bow which is heavier than it should be and will, therefore, never be coped with properly.

Field archers generally use bows of heavier weight than those of target archers, to take advantage of the flatter trajectory when shooting without sights. They will be using a style that on average draws an inch or two more than the target style so the formula still applies to them and gives that little extra weight they seek.

Draw length

The formula can only be accurately applied when the archer has learned to shoot and reached that level of competence in which the draw length has been established and is consistent. The simple test to determine the safe length of arrow is not going to be sufficiently accurate to calculate bow weight, so to overcome this, selections of bows could be made using the chart provided in this section. The draw length referred to is the distance from the back of the bow to the chin or reference point and is *not* the arrow length.

The draw length can be established by using a piece of dowel capable of being fitted to the bow string and marked

5. Establishing draw length.

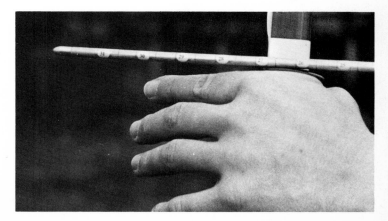

off in half inch steps around the anticipated draw length measured from the nock. An observer can see (when standing behind the archer and viewing the bow from the side) which of the marks coincides with the back of the bow. An average of ten such readings should be taken and the length determined will be accurate enough to enable the following chart to be used:

Draw length (Not arrow length)	Maximum recommended bow draw weight (pounds)		Recommended bow length (inches)		Recommended arrow tube number	
Inches	Men	Women	Target	Field	Men	Women
24	36	26	60	60	1518	1416
24½	37	27	62	60	1518	1516
25	37½	27½	64	62	1616	1518
25½	38	28	66	64	1616	1616
26	39	28½	66	64	1716	1616
26½	40	29	68	66	1816	1716
27	40½	29½	68	66	1816	1716
27½	41	30	68	68	1816	1716
28	42	30½	68	68	1816	1716
28½	42	31	70	68	1916	1816
29	43½	31½	70	70	1916	1816
29½	44	32	70	70	1916	1816
30	45	33	70	70	2016	1916
	These figures should be reduced a few pounds for the very slender person to avoid overbowing.		The shorter bows will give better cast on average and deliver the arrow on a flatter trajectory.		The first two figures are tube diameter in 64ths of an inch – the seconds are wall thickness of tube in thousands of an inch.	

There is another factor to be considered now that the bow draw weight has been decided, and that is the design of the bow in relation to the person who is going to use it.

Types of bow

Short bows, which can be considered as up to 62 inches in length, are fast in shooting and give very good cast. Longer bows, say 68 inches and above, tend to be slower in shooting.

The short bow is usually more sensitive or critical to shoot while the longer bows are usually smoother and more tolerant of error.

A short archer can get good results from using a short bow and often needs the better cast these bows give since with a very short arrow and relatively light bow this may be needed to reach the maximum distances eventually to be shot.

The archer of average height, using a longer bow, will have a draw length which produces a draw weight adequate to cope with the maximum championship distances. However, the tall and slender type of archer who has elected to shoot a bow a pound or two less than the figures given in the chart may need a bow of good cast to reach the maximum distances. The ideal would seem to be a short bow, but the draw length limit may well be small and the angle around the fingers formed by the string would be acute to the point of discomfort.

Referring back to the drawing of the composite bow, you will see that the centre section of the bow is called the riser section and it is to this non-moving section of the bow that the working limbs are attached.

By variation on the length of the riser section it is possible for the modern bow manufacturer to produce bows with a wide range of length and retain the advantages of the short working limbs.

So, the selection comes down to choosing a bow with a good length of riser section and relatively short working limb for the tall and slender, and a short riser section for the smaller person. The eventual selection will depend on pocket and preference, of course, but the above points form a basis upon which to make your decision.

Arrows

It is to be regretted that wooden arrows are still manufactured and offered for sale. These tend to shed their points (piles), may be broken easily, or worse can crack and then fold up at the moment of shooting, spraying slivers of wood in all directions. Wooden arrows should be *avoided* even as a gift!

The best ones are the aluminium tubular type. With these there is no danger of the arrow collapsing like a cracked wooden one, and they are made in such a way as to make them much more durable. They do not tend to shed their piles and the nock which fits onto the bow string is usually made of plastic or nylon and can easily be replaced. The grades of the aluminium tube do vary and the cheaper arrows, perfectly suitable for the beginner, tend to be softer in quality than the relatively more expensive tournament quality.

Pile

The pile of the arrow is usually made of steel, sometimes with a bullet shaped point and sometimes with a conical point. Experienced archers generally consider that the bullet shaped point is best.

Nock

The other end of the arrow shaft fitted with the nock may be formed into a conical point over which the nock is fixed with adhesive. Another type of arrow has a hollow end and the nock is inserted and either screwed in or glued in place.

The latter type can suffer from having the end of the tube split open if damage occurs to the nock. It then has to be replaced. So on balance, the 'cone end' nock fitting is preferable.

The nocks themselves vary in design, both to suit the type of attachment employed, i.e. coned or spigot end, and in respect of shape. Some have a ridge on one side which can be arranged to coincide with the cock feather on the arrow. This is favoured by hunters because the arrow relationship to the bow string can be identified by feeling the position of the ridge without having to take the eyes off the game to be shot. These are called index nocks. The mid nocks are another type which are without any indicating ridge of any kind and are normally used by target archers since they have time to look at what they are doing and don't need any index.

A further type of nock in common use these days is the keyhole-type which are designed to clip over the string with a positive action which some archers regard as a great benefit. The choice of nock design is a matter of preference, the mid nock and keyhole-type being equally suitable for target and field archery.

Fletchings and vanes

The fletchings or feathers on an arrow are most important and their relative position to the nock is significant. Three fletchings are usually equally distributed on the shaft with the cock feather position at 90° to the bow string – the other two are flight feathers, not hen feathers, as is often mistakenly believed.

Four feather fletchings are quite common on tournament arrows which have been fletched by their owners, and in

Three- and four-fletched arrows.

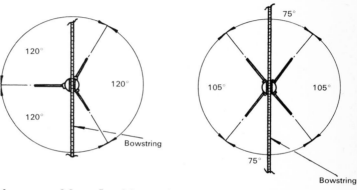

the case of four fletchings, they are not distributed equally around the shaft as this would give only 90° spacing. That *could* lead to fletchings fouling the arrow pass on the bow during shooting, which would deflect the arrow. To illustrate these comparisons, look at these two arrows drawn as if looking at the end of the arrow directly at the nock – the thick line represents the relative position of the bow string.

The reader may be wondering why, if the arrow rests on the side of the bow, the fletchings do not foul the bow? The fact is that the arrow does not move in a straight line when it is shot. A phenomenon called the 'archers paradox' operates. The nock of the arrow is accelerated by the bow string when it is released, before the tip of the arrow begins to move. Something has to give, of course, and what happens is that the arrow deflects towards the centre of the bow. This takes only microseconds to happen, the arrow then moves forward, but having been bent, it then flexes in the opposite direction. This oscillation continues in the arrow for some distance after being shot and is damped out by the action of the fletchings, which is what they are for. The diagram illustrates this sequence of events.

By having arrows of the appropriate flexibility or spine

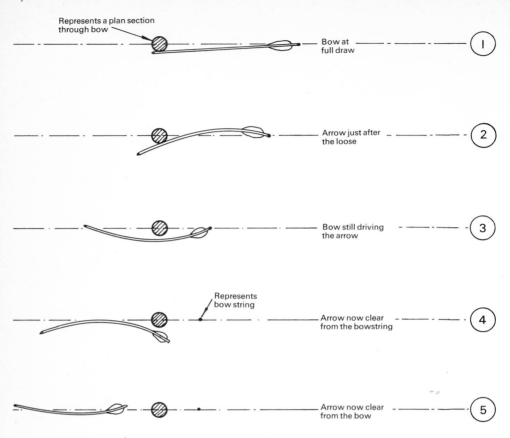

Represents a plan section through bow

Bow at full draw — 1

Arrow just after the loose — 2

Bow still driving the arrow — 3

Represents bow string

Arrow now clear from the bowstring — 4

Arrow now clear from the bow — 5

The archer's paradox.

Arrow will continue to bend until fletchings finally damp out all movement—the arrow should bend enough to make the fletchings clear the bow—excessive bend in the arrow could cause it to fly to the right of the centre of the target.

we can *use* this oscillation to *ensure* that the fletchings never touch the bow and this means the arrows are matched to the bow. Remember that word matched as we shall meet it again soon!

Since the arrow fletchings do not, or should not, touch the bow it is soon obvious that an artificial rigid vane could be used to replace the feather as a means of fletching and this is now the case, as most target archers now use plastic vanes. These are regarded as more consistent than feathers, since being man-made they are exact duplicates of each other in a given set, whereas no two feathers are exactly the same. The plastic vanes are not effected by damp in the way feathers can be, which is another advantage.

Field archers do need rather larger stabilizing surfaces than target archers, since the damping action needs to take place more rapidly, due to the shorter ranges being shot over. Heavier bows tend to be used, hence heavier arrows and more effort in damping out the oscillation is required.

We now know that the bow's energy will cause the arrow to 'bend' and for accurate shooting it is vital that all the arrows behave exactly the same way in this respect. In other words, they must be matched to the bow and to each other and are, therefore, described as a matched set of arrows. This means that they are all the same length, the same weight, the same diameter and tube wall thickness and have the same piles and nocks.

However, in the early stages a purchased set of modestly priced practice arrows will come fully fitted and well matched to meet standards more exacting than the new archer is liable to exceed for some time. The chart of bow weights earlier in the chapter gives arrow tube code numbers suitable for the weight of bow you intend to use.

Tab

Perhaps the most personal item of equipment in the archer's tackle is the shooting tab. The purpose of the shooting tab is to cover the string fingers so that the surface of the tab is between the bow's string and the finger tips. This produces a consistent surface from which the string will be released and helps to produce a consistent result also. Shooting could be done without a tab but eventually the pressure on the tips of the fingers would make them sore and the quality of control of the string would suffer. The surface of the fingers do not remain constant, since temperature changes produce variations in the degree of surface moisture on the skin.

The most suitable kind of tab is the one illustrated in the photograph which has been cut to fit the archer who owns it and beside it is shown the untrimmed tab as a comparison.

This type of tab has the finger holes arranged to fit over the second and third fingers, as these are the ones that do the work when the bow is drawn and the top of the index finger is free. Some fit on the top and third fingers, but these are rather clumsy and uncomfortable and are best avoided.

The tab has to be trimmed and the slot for the arrow nock needs to be widened. Initially the tab should be

6. *Left* Untrimmed tab. *Right* Tab trimmed to fit the archer.

trimmed so that when the tab is fitted to the fingers and the fingers are straight, the material reaches to the finger tips – this can be reduced later on when the action of loosing is perfected, but for the moment the little bit of extra length will keep the tips of the fingers protected from the soreness resulting from an occasional bad loose, in the early stages.

The arrow slot need only be large enough to clear the nock of the arrow on the bow string and the minimum cut away to achieve this is the ideal.

The upper edge of the tab should be trimmed to follow the index finger so that it coincides with the edge of the finger but does not project beyond it. This helps with the 'under chin' anchor sensation of the target archer and the reference point of the field archer is more easily located without an excess of material in that position.

A tab is often made of pony butt or skin which gives excellent results. It has one smooth side, which enables a good surface to be presented to the bow string.

The surface of the tab needs to be sealed against moisture so that shooting in wet weather is nor affected, at least by the tab. This can be done by immersing the whole tab in a shallow dish of silicone furniture polish and leaving it overnight. In the morning, avoid wiping off the excess and

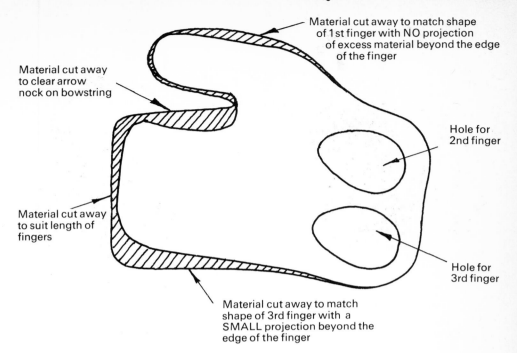

Material cut away to match shape of 1st finger with NO projection of excess material beyond the edge of the finger

Material cut away to clear arrow nock on bowstring

Hole for 2nd finger

Material cut away to suit length of fingers

Hole for 3rd finger

Material cut away to match shape of 3rd finger with a SMALL projection beyond the edge of the finger

A new finger tab trimmed to fit the archer's hand.

hang it up for twenty-four hours to dry. Then take a medium to stiff brush and burnish off the excess polish and you have a very smooth waterproof tab which will last for some considerable time. Tabs can be purchased in materials other than pony butt. A number of man-made materials under various trade names have been marketed and have proved most successful.

One type is the hair surface tab which is excellent to shoot with and does not deteriorate when wet. Tabs of this type do wear rather quickly however, and this needs to be taken into account when making the choice as the tab will need to be replaced more often.

Bracer

The bracer is the device worn on the inside of the bow arm between the wrist and the elbow. Its purpose is to keep the loose material in the sleeves of the clothing out of the path of the bow string. Almost any design which meets that requirement can be considered suitable and there is a wide variety to choose from on the market. Whatever type is chosen it should not restrict the movement of either wrist or elbow and, of course, must have straps or clips which will fit well without restricting the blood circulation.

The bow string, when shot, should never contact the bow arm, but we do know that when the arrow has left the bowstring, the string bounce makes the centre of the string move on an elliptical path which could lead to it touching the inner fore-arm. It is desirable, then, to wear the bracer even when bare-armed in warm weather.

Quivers

When not actually shooting, such as when collecting arrows, some form of storage device upon which to place the bow is desirable and a good bow stand or ground quiver is useful. This applies to target archery rather than field archery since in the latter the bow is carried forward to the target when scoring and collecting in preparation for the move on to the next target.

A ground quiver has the added feature of providing a

7. A selection of quivers.

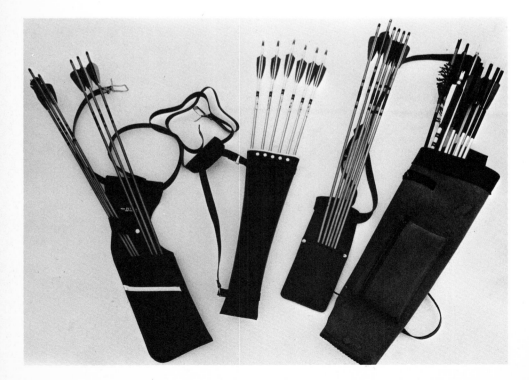

storage place for the arrows, and makes a good marker to indicate the shooting position during training.

Later on, of course, the archer will be required in competition archery to move back from the the shooting line taking the bow, and the ground quiver is then used behind the waiting line.

There are many designs of ground quiver, but a suitable one with the bow hung on it and arrows stowed is shown in the photograph.

Many archers prefer to use a belt or pocket quiver in target archery and some form of quiver which is worn is essential in field archery as you are more mobile in that discipline.

There are many types of good quivers available and some excellent examples are shown in the illustration.

Foot markers

Target archers need to maintain a precise standing position which they have to leave and return to during the course of shooting, so means of marking the position of the feet is essential.

The International Rules of Shooting permit the use of foot markers that do not project above the ground more than 1 cm, but even at that height they can be accidentally kicked out of position by other archers.

Perhaps the best kind are those made in the form of a flat disc of plastic or aluminium with a spike a couple of

A suitable foot marker (one of a pair).

The pin head and disc can be coloured to choice. Dimensions quoted are for guidance only and can be varied—total projection above ground level must not exceed 1 cm ($\frac{3}{8}''$).

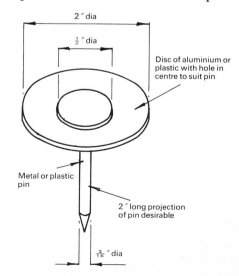

2″ dia

$\frac{1}{2}$″ dia

Disc of aluminium or plastic with hole in centre to suit pin

Metal or plastic pin

2″ long projection of pin desirable

$\frac{3}{16}$″ dia

inches long which can be pressed into the ground to go down flush with the surface. The diagram shows such a foot marker and, of course, a pair would be needed.

Other equipment

The third group of items of equipment you may need concerns additional extras which are very desirable. The Field archer has a natural break in mental concentration in that the move from one target to another gives a change of scene, a change of target and in general, a change of interest.

The target archer enjoys none of these and *must* introduce a break in the sequence in order to rest the mind and body to ensure adequate powers of concentration when actually shooting. Target archers shoot three arrows then retire from the shooting position to return later to shoot another set of three arrows. This is a sequence that provides for archers shooting in company, to change over after each set of three arrows.

Chair

An opportunity exists to take a rest, for which a comfortable light folding chair is needed. The chair should have an adequate height of backrest and should give good support to the spine. Arm rests are usually provided on such chairs, but these are not essential. A folding stool without a backrest is not as good as a chair, since the back cannot be rested and a slumped posture on a stool spoils the breathing action. These points will be developed later in the final chapter of this book.

Binoculars

By no means essential, a pair of binoculars can be very useful when shooting longer distances so a close-up of how the arrows are landing can be obtained. Certainly they will not be needed in the early days as the distances will be modest to begin with.

Tackle box

A decent tackle box is a 'must', to carry such items of equipment as arrows, bracer, tab, foot markers, spare bow string, or strings, a spool of serving thread, a few spare nocks and

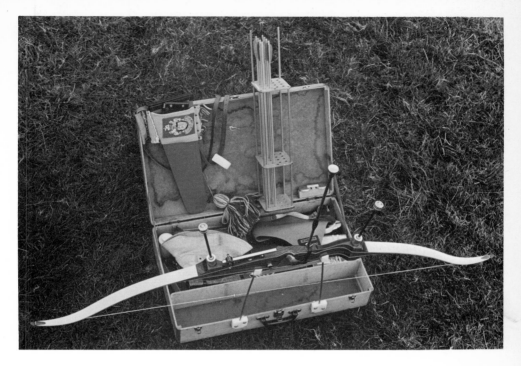

8. A typical tackle box.

a tube of adhesive. A measuring device to check the bracing height of the bow will be needed and this will normally remain in the tackle box. (Bracing height is the distance from the bow string to a selected point on the bow and is fully explained in the next chapter.)

The field archers cannot be expected to lug a tackle box all round the course with them so they will tend to carry some useful spares in the numerous pockets so often provided on the more elaborate back quiver or belt quiver they might purchase. Most archers tend to make their own tackle box. It can be designed to carry what they want and the author has been amazed by the sheer volume of hardware some archers seem to feel the need for. Tackle maintenance, properly carried out, could mean most of the junk being left at home.

Bow bag

The bow needs to be taken care of and if it is a conventional one piece bow (some are take-apart, and have a case) it will need a bow bag of canvas or plastic to contain it, when not in use. When not supplied with the bow, this also can be made at modest cost, or purchased, and resembles a fishing rod bag.

Your tackle and equipment all represent an investment worth treating with care and if used and .maintained properly will last a long time and give good service.

Clothing

Clothing worn for archery should be close fitting without restricting movement (see Chapter 3) and various colours are designated by some countries. The GNAS in Great Britain, for example, require green or white or a combination of the two. Certain regulations in FITA rules insist that competing ladies wear dresses or skirts and suitable tops and gentlemen full length slacks and long or short sleeved shirts. Sweaters and cardigans may be worn and in adverse weather suitable protective clothing.

For field archery ladies are permitted to wear trouser suits or slacks instead of skirts.

Other items

A useful accessory is an umbrella, either hand held or capable of being fixed by its own stake into the ground. For cold weather shooting, some archers purchase handwarmers which are devices capable of generating heat to the surface of their outer case. A useful alternative is a pair of mittens to be worn when not actually shooting.

3 Before you start to shoot

The safe conduct of archery is of prime importance. The earlier chapters have mentioned that bows and arrows have been used for centuries for hunting and warfare, so it is obvious that they can kill people just as well today as they ever could. The archery world has always been very aware of safety observancies and conduct when handling archery tackle so accidents are extremely rare. This is an excellent sport which all can enjoy *but* if archers, or would be archers, fail to act with good sense, they could cease to be sportsmen and become a menace to all around them.

Remember one cardinal rule as far as safety is concerned; being reasonably sure won't do – be certain.

Shooting range layout

In target archery, ample space must be left behind targets; at least 50 yards (50 metres) overshoot must be allowed. On either side of the target or group of targets at least 30 yards (30 metres) should be allowed. Targets should never be set up in any position where there is a chance of a passer-by being at risk. They should not be set up so that the arrows would be travelling towards buildings, gardens or public pathways or roads.

When it is impossible to have an isolated area, then the overshoot and side clearances should be enclosed in a roped off area with warning signs posted at approach points such as footpaths. The shooting position for each target should be clearly marked on the shooting line, and all archers when not shooting should retire behind a waiting line marked out 5 yards (5 metres) to the rear of the shooting line. Visitors should not be permitted to come closer than 10 yards (10 metres) behind the waiting line and any side ropes should extend back as far as the visitors line.

Indoor shooting

When shooting indoors, entrances other than those behind the shooting line must be secured against people suddenly walking through into danger.

Back stop netting, or a similar protection should be arranged behind the targets to stop any arrows that miss. The damage to a wall (or the arrow) is one thing, but it is not unknown for arrows to bounce back off a wall for a good 25 yards distance.

No one should be watching archery from the side-lines when indoors – all should be behind the shooting line. It is not always possible to arrange waiting lines and visitors lines when indoors but observe the spirit of that rule.

With respect to field archery, the author would caution a novice against attempting to lay out a field course. It takes experience to avoid inadvertently putting someone's shooting position in line with the overshoot from another target. Field courses are progressive as has been mentioned before and must be laid out in the *absolute certainty* that all positions of targets, shooting positions. and pathways are safe, without neglecting public pathways in the area.

Targets

The targets themselves demand attention in respect of safety. It would be very damaging to the arrows if a boss fell off a stand, or were blown off. It may even be pulled off by an archer withdrawing arrows incorrectly, with dire consequences if the boss full of arrows were to fall on someone.

The target stands should be inspected before use to ensure that all the timber is sound, that the supports for the boss are strong and have not worked loose. Each leg of the stand should have a spike to secure it from spreading when on the ground. Guy ropes should be permanently attached and set out when the target stand is erected. When used indoors, some method of securing the feet of the stand is needed. A shallow wooden triangular frame is best (the spikes should be removed of course), or at a pinch, ropes to restrict the spread of the legs would do. The target boss should be tied, or otherwise adequately secured, to the target stand and it is best fixed at or near the apex of the legs and near both supports. The observation of these measures will provide a safe place to shoot, so now it would be wise to check the equipment.

The bow

The bow should be examined now and looked over to ensure that the whole length is free from cracks or splits. Examine the string nocks at either end to ensure they are both sound and smooth to accept the loops of the bow string. Some solid glass-fibre bows have added-on handles of rubber or plastic which can slip out of position. Check and correct this and secure with adhesive or tape. If the bow is fitted with a sight then check that the sight track is secure and if a pin is being used to aim with, see that it is tucked away in the top of the foam with the point well buried. The bow string should now be examined, and it is easy to see a loose or broken strand when the string is not under tension. A furry or fluffy appearance should also be an indication that the string should be rejected as it will soon break.

If all is well so far, examine the loops at each end of the string to see that these are still well protected by the tough outer serving and are not pulling apart where the sides of the loop join the main body of the string. Then check the centre serving for security, and finally examine the nocking point. It should be secure and give a clear indication of the nocking position.

Bracing the bow

When satisfied that both the bow and string are in good order, the bow can be braced, that is, the string placed in the shooting position. With a flat bow this is a simple matter once the know-how is acquired.

The bow is held in the left hand as shown in the photograph with the back uppermost and the tip of the bottom limb located in the welt of the left shoe and the right hand located on the upper limb. The right hand is arranged as shown in figure 10, ready to push the top loop of the string into the the upper string nock. Now pull the handle and push the upper limb, causing the bow to bend. Slide the

43

9. Preparing to
   brace the bow.

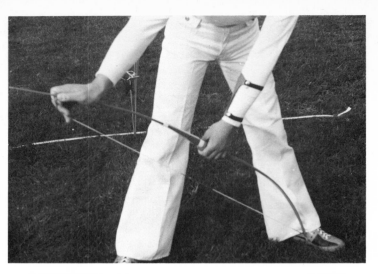

10. Sliding the
    string into place
    with the hand.

11. The pull and
    push action to
    bend the bow
    and slide the
    string into place.

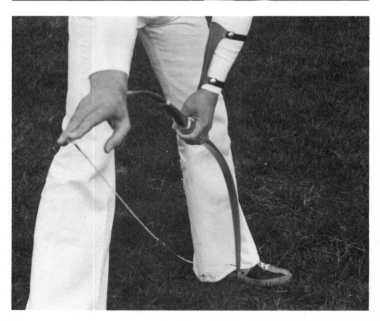

12. Checking to see that the string loops are secure.

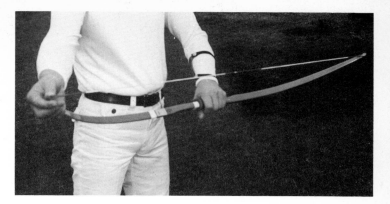

string, using the finger tips, into the groove and make sure it engages. Slowly relax the hands and the bow should be braced. Swing the bow up horizontally in front of you with the bow held away. If the string suddenly slips off one end you are not in a hazardous position when holding the bow in this manner. Keep the bow as above and inspect each end of the string to see that it is fully engaged in the nocks. The bow is now braced and can be hung on the bow stand (ground quiver).

To unbrace the bow the process is simply reversed, but some dexterity is required to manipulate the top loop out of position as when doing this the pressure of the hand to bend the bow has to be maintained. The hand position should be such as will prevent the bow, if it slips, flying up the inside of the arm.

13. The hand position when unbracing the bow.

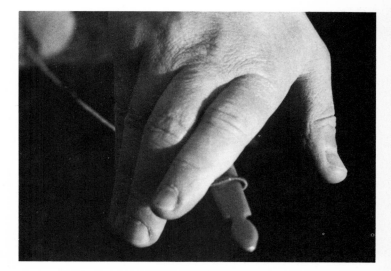

The fibre-glass bow with the reflex tips can be strung in the same manner as described above, but it is a little more difficult due to the shape of the tips. A simple 'bow stringer' can be made from a loop of soft rope and used in conjunction with a cup of the type used beneath chair castors, to receive the lower tip of the bow. This method, as shown, is easier for women in particular. If the bow to be strung is one of the composite type then a good bow stringer would be worth buying as it gives better protection to the bow and is easy to use. In this case both limbs of the bow are free of the ground and are not stressed in a manner liable to damage them. Whatever method is employed, do practise this well.

14. Rope, loop and cup method of bracing the bow.

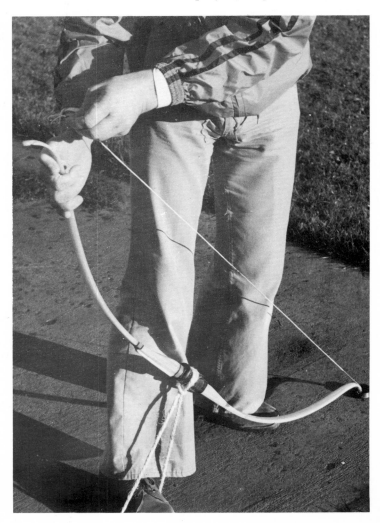

15. A composite bow and stringer in use.

Bracing height

Next, check the bracing height which on the fibre-glass bow is measured from the string to the back of the bow (i.e. the side of the bow furthest from the string) and on both types is about 8 inches (20 cm). The measurement may vary from one bow to another but should in any event be *constant*. If the bracing height varies, the cast or throwing power of the bow would be inconsistent. A gradual reduction or letting down of the bracing height would be a sign that the bow string is broken under some serving in a place where your check could not spot it.

A composite bow will probably have a larger bracing height but, again, it should be consistent. Deliberate variation of the bracing height, within limits, can be carried out as part of bow tuning, but this should not be attempted by the inexperienced as a bracing height set too low can damage the bow. It is a reasonable indication that the composite bow is not braced too low when there is some unoccupied string grove at each end of the limbs.

47

Arrows

Look for burrs or sharp barbs on the piles and file them off. Make sure all the piles are secure. Examine the nocks to ensure that they are all secure. Look at each leg of the nocks to make sure none are cracked and liable to break off and there are no barbs in between them.

The shafts of the arrows come next and should be examined for dents.

Any dent greater than one quarter of the diameter should not be accepted. The shafts need to be reasonably straight and this is best checked by spinning the arrow between the nails of finger and thumb. Those which are bent will jump out of the hand.

16. Spinning the arrow to check that it is straight.

Examine the fletchings to see that all are secure, and pay due attention to the front of the feather to see that it is glued well at that point and has no nasty barbs at the spine of the feather. Any found can be pared away with a sharp knife, or smoothed off by a pencil wrapped in sandpaper to make a rasp.

Personal checks

The equipment checks are now completed and personal checks come next. Depending on climatic conditions, clothing needs to be warm and comfortable but should be close fitting on the upper trunk, and in particular the arms. Badges and brooches or jewellery should be avoided as these could catch in the bow string with embarrassing results. Any scarves, or ties, if worn should be tucked out of the way. Some women like to tie a scarf around the neck with the tails flowing free. Very nice too, but deadly in archery!

Sensible shoes with low heels please! Field archers should wear stronger footwear since they are going over rough country and in some countries where snakes are about it may call for stout leggings to be worn as well. In any event, field archers should keep the legs covered if in very rough country to protect them from scratches. Please don't wear smooth soles on shoes or boots in field archery or you could easily slip and fall.

If you are a smoker, and you feel you must smoke when enjoying archery, put the pipe or cigarette in a safe place when shooting – *beware* in forest or dry grassland – cigarettes have been known to cause fires. Remember, use common sense.

Shooting

1 Never commence shooting without being *certain* that the range is clear.

2 Never point a loaded bow in any direction other than at the target.

3 Never point a drawn bow, even without an arrow, at anyone.

4 Never draw a bow beyond its intended limit.

5 Never loose a bow from full draw without an arrow in it; damage to the bow could occur.

6 Never shoot an arrow straight up in the air as no-one knows where it is going to come down.

7 Never take snap shots at anything in either Target or Field archery.

8 Never throw an arrow like a dart at anyone, nor jab at them with either the pile or the nock.

9 Always ensure when shooting with others that agreed signals are given before shooting begins, to make sure everyone is in a safe place and ready.

10 Never shoot from a position other than on the shooting line.

49

11 Always ensure that an agreed signal is given before anyone moves forward to collect or score. Have an agreed signal, such as the cry Fast, to be called out if anyone sees a dangerous situation develop.

12 Always walk to the target. Whenever possible walk to the left of centre so avoiding arrows that may have dropped short.

Never run

13 Always ensure that the others with you are not in a position to be jabbed in the face by arrows being pulled from the target boss or butt.

14 Always support the target face with the back of one hand and gently push away while pulling the arrow out straight with the other hand. Hold the arrow close to the target to avoid bending it.

15 Always, in Field archery, when searching for lost

17. Withdrawing arrows.

arrows, lay a bow across the face of the target to indicate that people are about and the target is *not yet clear*.

16 Always keep dogs on leads and control children who may not be aware of the dangers obvious to adults.

4 How to shoot – target archery

This chapter contains a logical method of progress towards shooting your first arrow, and the time taken to do this from when the shooting area has been prepared is only about a quarter of an hour.

The target

The reader may recall from Chapter 1 that this form of archery is carried out on a suitable area of ground which would contain one or more targets arranged on stands and shot at from fixed distances. These vary from 90 metres down to 30 metres for the International Round (the shorter distance being shot on the smaller 80 cm target face) and from 100 yards down to 40 yards on the popular traditional rounds.

To try to start shooting at these distances would be quite unsatisfactory as the initial accuracy may not be good enough to even hit the target. Start 20 yards (or 20 metres) from the shooting position to begin with and set up the target and stand, taking care to maintain the safety observvancies described in Chapter 3.

Which way round to shoot

About 75 per cent of the population are right-handed and the rest left-handed or ambidextrous and this will have an influence on the position adopted for shooting. A right-handed person will normally use the right hand for the delicate or manipulative types of movement such as writing, and would use the left hand for more passive activity (such as holding a loaf of bread when using the bread knife in the right hand).

When shooting, it is desirable to use the higher degree of manipulative skill of the right hand for the relatively delicate task of controlling the arrow on the bow string and use the left hand for the more passive holding of the bow.

The reverse would be true of a left-handed person. The

ambidextrous person can choose either way but even he would tend to use one hand more than the other – in writing, for example, and this should influence his choice.

The aiming eye

As will be realized as this chapter develops, the nock end of the arrow will be located under the chin and one eye will be used to aim the arrow at the target. Just as the majority of people have one hand dominant so it can be that one eye may be dominant. This does not mean that when this condition exists there is anything wrong with the eyes, but it is important to ensure that this situation cannot have an adverse effect on aiming at the target.

To ensure this cannot happen, the *non*-aiming eye could be closed during the portion of the shooting technique concerned, thus even if the *non*-aiming eye were the dominant one (or when no dominance exists) the non-aiming eye cannot influence the aim. An alternative method of doing this is to cover the non-aiming eye with an eye patch of an opaque material that will admit light, but not allow complete vision. This has the effect of giving dominance to the aiming eye without the other eye having to be closed. Spectacle wearers can obtain a clip-on device for this purpose.

Fitting the equipment

The bracer, the quiver and tab can now be fitted. The tab would slide over the second and third fingers of the right hand for a right-handed person with the slot to clear the arrow nock positioned between the first and second fingers.

The tab should have been trimmed to ensure that no material projects beyond the finger tips and the arrow slot will often need to be modified slightly to ensure that the widest part of the slot is extended as far as the second joint of the index finger. This will prevent the tab interfering with the arrow nock when the arrow and the finger come together on the bow string.

Fit the bracer on the bow arm, checking that it does not restrict the free movement of either the wrist or the elbow and that the fixing straps are secure without being overtight.

Standing position

We will discuss the situation for the right-handed person so the opposite will apply for a left-handed person. The standing position is very important as it is the base from which all that follows takes place. The archer needs to ensure that a line through the shoulders passes through the vertical centre line of the target when the body is in a comfortable standing position. Begin by placing the feet about shoulder width apart, one foot either side of the shooting position (or shooting line if there is one) with the left side of the body towards the target and the right side away from the target. Don't try to adopt a sergeant major-type of posture, stand upright but relaxed with the eyes on the horizon.

Ensure that your foot markers are within comfortable reach!

18. The standing position.

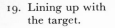

19. Lining up with
the target.

Extend both arms to reach out in line and level with the
shoulders and with both hands making a fist with the
knuckles on top. Turn the head (with the left eye closed)
and note the position of the second knuckle of the left fist
in relation to the centre of the target. It is probable that
the knuckle will appear to be to the right or left of the
centre of the target so, maintaining the position of the arms,
shuffle both feet around until the knuckle is lined up with
the centre of the target. Relax with the arms down and turn
the head to the front again.

Check that the new standing position is still comfortable
with the feet still about shoulder width apart, and then
without looking, raise both arms as before. Close the left eye

and turn the head to check that your position has not changed. When you are satisfied with your standing position, place the foot markers at the tip of each toe of your shoe and push them into the ground. You can now leave and return to the correct standing position whenever necessary without constant checking.

What the setting up has done, is aim your body at the target which is vital to the achievement of good technique allied to accuracy.

The ground quiver can now be fixed in position a comfortable reach in front of your standing position (or the belt quiver fitted) and the arrows can be placed in the quiver – start off with three arrows for the time being.

The bow

The next step is to prepare the bow which should be braced as described (and by now practised) in Chapter 3.

20. Fixing the position of the sight pin.

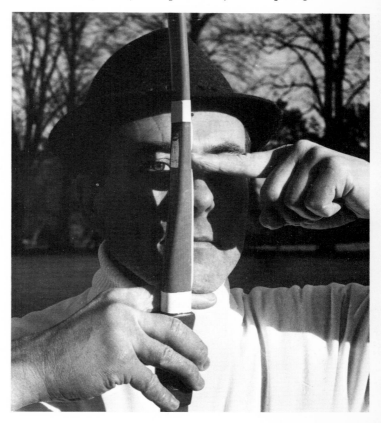

21. Sight pin in
place.

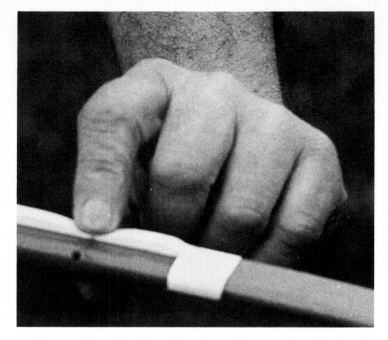

The position for the sight pin, still stowed safely in the top of the foam strip, is now to be determined and this is done by placing the bow against the face with a finger between the chin and the part of the handle upon which the arrow will rest, known as the arrow shelf. With the free hand identify the position on the foam strip that corresponds with the centre of the eye. Move the bow away from the face and take the pin from the top of the foam and insert it into the side of the foam strip, so that the plastic head is just projecting beyond the edge of the bow on the same side as the arrow shelf, that is, the left side of the bow for a right-handed archer. Place the bow on the bow hooks of the ground quiver or place it in a suitable position on the ground in front of the standing position.

Checking head position

Re-assume the standing position, using the foot markers, and take one of the arrows from the quiver. Hold the pointed end (the pile end) of the arrow between thumb and forefinger of the right hand, and hold the arrow upright against the face touching the tip of the nose and front centre of the chin. It is important that the mouth is shut during this check. Cover or close the left eye and turn the head slowly to the target and adjust the head position until the blurred image of the arrow appears to cut down the centre of the target in a vertical line.

Without moving the head, take the arrow away and see the unrestricted view of the target in relation to the bridge of the nose (left eye still covered or closed). Repeat this check a number of times until satisfied that you can repeat the position *without* using the arrow as a guide.

This action will not only help you to turn your head the the correct amount, but it will also have tilted the head so that the right eye, the aiming eye as it will be, is positioned vertically over the centre of the chin. This position is very important and worth a little extra effort to perfect it.

Holding the bow

Take up the bow in the left hand and position the string uppermost between the arm and body so that the string is in the vicinity of the bracer with the fingers cupping the handle and the thumb on top pointing up the limb of the bow.

22. Initial hand position.

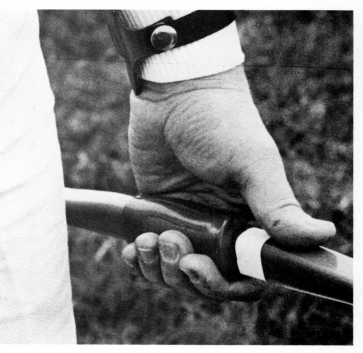

23. Final hand
    position.

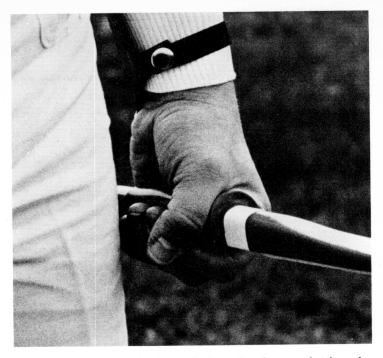

Drop the thumb down and close the fingers, letting the
arm hang loosely down the side of the body. The hand
should close around the handle of the bow with the sort of
feeling one would have if carrying an empty suitcase. The
bow handle should never be gripped under any circumstances.

Positioning the bow arm

Turn the head towards the target (both eyes may be open
for this) and raise the bow arm level with the shoulder
(similar to setting up the standing position) with the bow
held in a horizontal position in the hand. The arm will be
extended but the elbow joint should *not* be stiff and locked.

Without moving the elbow joint, rotate the wrist to
bring the bow to the vertical position. You should now see
a gap of about $\frac{3}{4}$ in (2 cm) between the forearm and the bow
string. If there is no such gap, check that the elbow has not
extended to the locked position, then provided the elbow is
not locked, repeat the movement of the wrist from horizontal to vertical.

If the gap is still not present, the bow hand should be

adjusted on the handle of the bow to create the gap and the whole arm-raising, wrist-turning, test carried out until a satisfactory position has been confirmed.

The position of the bow arm extended but not locked at the elbow, and the bow held upright with a good string clearance, is the same as the relationship which should exist in the bow arm when the full draw position is reached and during the subsequent aiming and releasing of the arrow. It is an important one to get right.

Nocking the arrow

Swing the bow arm and the bow around the body at waist level approximately, with the wrist moved a little to present the bow in an accessible position to fit the arrow to the string: this is termed nocking the arrow.

Take one arrow from the quiver and hold it between the thumb and fingers of the shaft hand around that part of the arrow where the coloured bands lie below the fletchings.

Lay the arrow across the bow and rotate it, if required, to bring the cock feather uppermost. Push the nock end of the arrow onto the string at the nocking point.

Placing the fingers on the string

Fold the finger tab into the palm for the moment. Place the second and third fingers of the shaft hand onto the string to the left of the arrow nock with a gap of about $\frac{1}{8}$ inch (3 mm) between the second finger and the arrow. The string should lie in the creases of the first joint of both fingers, which for most people will mean slightly crooking the second finger (the one nearest the arrow) to bring the creases in line and the *fingers at 90° to the bow string*.

Next, push the bow hand away a couple of inches – this will cause the bow string to apply a little pressure to the fingers on the string, the tips of which should then be slightly crooked upwards. The finger tips will then be seen to bunch up as little pads of flesh in front of the bow string, which will hold it securely.

Now place the first finger on the string, to the right of the arrow and in contact with it. The crease in the finger will probably not reach the string but this is quite satisfactory

24. Placing the fingers on the string.

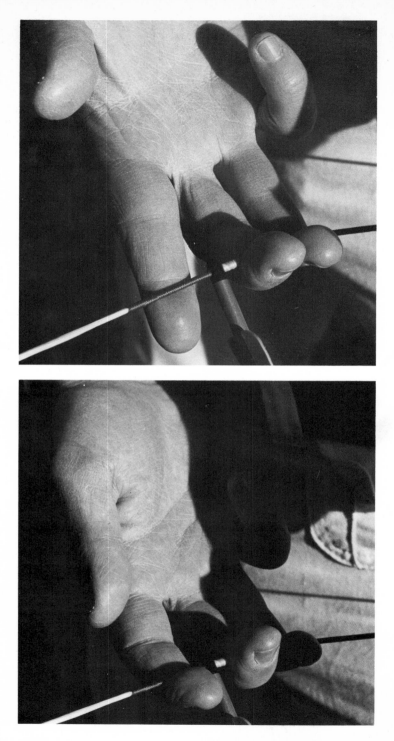

25. First finger in place on the string.

26. The tab in
    place.

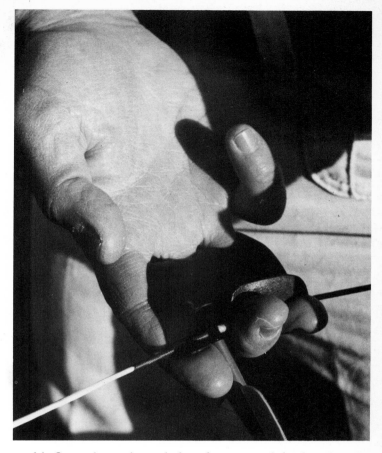

as this finger is not intended to do any work in drawing the
bow.

Repeat this process several times until fully confident
that it is being carried out correctly, and then bring the
finger tab into position on the fingers and repeat the
exercise with the tab in place. The tab will make the
pressure on the finger tips less apparent and you must
concentrate on ensuring that the second and third fingers
are correctly engaged on the bow string, just clear of the
arrow ($\frac{1}{8}$ in or 3 mm remember) and that the first finger is in
contact with the arrow but not applying any pressure to the
string.

The fingers on the string, the palm of the hand and the
wrist joint should all be sufficiently relaxed to allow a
straight line to form through the arrow and right through
to the elbow of the shaft arm.

27. The low
preparation
position, note
the relaxed
shaft hand.

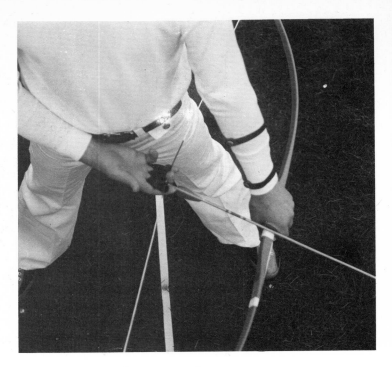

Loosing into the ground

The action of releasing the arrow after aiming at the target
is first practised by shooting into the ground a few yards
ahead of the shooting position. This enables the archer to
appreciate the action of the loose, as it is called, and see how
it works. This prepares for the stage of shooting at the target
when the action cannot be seen by the archer. Nock an
arrow on the bow string and place the fingers in position,
using the tab of course, and push the bow away initially.
Move the elbow in the opposite direction to the bow hand,
which will cause the shaft hand to follow and draw the bow
about 8 inches (20 cm). Do not be tempted to *pull* the string
back with the shaft hand as this will bring the wrong
muscles into play. Hold this position for a few seconds and
then draw the string back another inch or so *and at the same
time* straighten the finger tips on the bow string.

The arrow will fly and stick in the ground a few yards
away. Repeat this with the other two arrows from the
quiver and continue after recovering them each time to
shoot a couple of dozen times until fully confident that the
loosing action is understood.

28. A coach's view of the preparation line. He should observe the straight line from the shaft arm elbow right through to the arrow pile.

29. Partly drawn bow, in preparation for ground loosing.

Drawing the bow

This is accomplished in stages and is commenced by nocking an arrow and placing the fingers on the string as before, then check that the bow arm is not locked at the elbow and the visual check on fingers and string, wrist, etc. shows that all are as they should be. When satisfied, assume a comfortable standing position with the head in the frontal position. Cover or close the non-aiming eye and turn the head towards the target, as previously practised, and fix the gaze on the centre of the target. (This is the low preparation position.)

30. The high preparation position.

Now raise the bow arm and the shaft arm letting both wrists rotate in unison to turn the bow upright and bring both hands a little above shoulder level. (This is the high preparation position.) If the arrow tends to fall off the bow during the draw, ensure that the shaft hand is not coming up too quickly so as to be in advance of the bow hand. The reverse would be acceptable. Next, push the bow arm towards the target and press the shaft arm elbow in the opposite direction which will begin drawing the bow. The bow arm will descend to be level with the shoulder while the shaft hand should move to bring the bow string in contact with the face, touching the front centre of the chin

31. Full draw position.

and the nose. The first finger of the shaft hand should be touching the underside of the chin.

If the string is not touching the nose, tilt the head forward until it does. Come down to the low preparation position and repeat the drawing practice until the action feels smooth and reasonably comfortable.

Remember to separate each action, don't turn the head at the same time as raising the bow, for instance, keep them as separate actions; this helps you to learn them correctly. Keep your gaze fixed on the target all the time after turning the head. Learn to 'feel' rather than 'see' the movements. Make quite sure when you have the bow at full draw that the elbow of the bow arm is not locked and that both shoulders are comfortable and relaxed, just as they were feeling before the bow was drawn.

If the arrow length has been selected in accordance with the advice given in Chapter 2 there should not be any risk of an overdraw; that is, when the pile of the arrow comes back further than the arrow pass and drops onto the bow hand on the belly side of the bow. Should this occur, however, it is VITAL to keep the bow at FULL DRAW and *lean forward* to let the arrow pile swing clear and *then* slowly let the bow string down to bracing height, controlling with the shaft hand.

32. Overdrawn arrow.

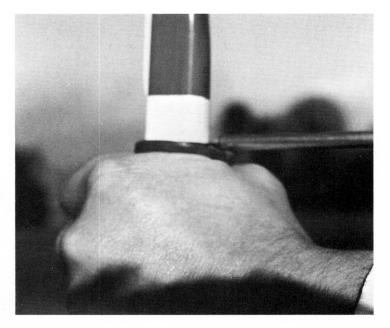

33. The position to adopt if an overdraw occurs.

Aiming

When the position of full draw is attained you should be able to see the target with the gold on or near the same side as the sight pin and and the blurred image of the bow string should be observed to be within the width of the bow limb.

Now observe the sight pin and where it is in relation to the target gold. If it is above or below the centre of the target, then bring the sight pin into the centre by moving the whole of the upper trunk from the waist, taking care *not* to alter the relative positions of the arms to the shoulders. *It will not do* just to raise or lower the bow arm as this upsets the whole balance of the full draw position. The sight pin should now be within the area of the gold. It is not necessary to try to hold the bow steadier than is required to keep the aim within the gold. The sight pin can be allowed to move around a little. To try to maintain a rock steady position is impossible at this stage. Even when experienced, one is never rock steady but the amount of movement will be smaller.

67

The aim is now established and can be repeated as a practice but should never be regarded as the signal to shoot.

Do not be tempted to look directly at the bow, the sight pin or the string, but rather see them in secondary vision when observing their positions and keep the aiming eye focused on the target centre.

N.B. If the centre of the target does not appear near the edge of the bow when at full draw, don't twist the body to correct it – instead refer to 'Correcting the Aim'. (Page 87.)

Should the blurred image of the bow string not be within the width of the bow limb then this indicates that the head position is incorrect. Ensure that the string is touching the tip of the nose and centre of the chin with the first finger of the shaft hand touching underneath, then tilt the head a little as follows:—

(a) If the string is beyond the width of the limb to the left, then tilt the top of the head to the left.
(b) If the string is beyond the width of the limb to the right then tilt the top of the head to the right.

The string will then seem to move and is correct when it appears within the width of the bow limb.

Holding

This period is the time between taking aim and loosing the arrow at the target. It is the period for settling down into a comfortable full draw position and aiming at the target.

Provided that the previous instructions have been carried out correctly the full draw should feel comfortable after a little practice and the load across the shoulders should feel balanced.

It is the large muscles of the back and shoulders which are intended to carry the load. When an uncomfortable cramped up or unbalanced feeling is experienced, this is a clear indication that the correct muscles are not being employed. Should that occur, return to the low preparation position and start again. Never continue when you don't feel right. Concentrate on the feeling of pushing the chest out when reaching the last few inches of the full draw position which will help to put the load on the correct muscles and bring the shoulders back as they should be.

Establish the aim and the hold position to settle down. This deliberate pause between taking aim and loosing is called the hold and is most important as it allows the whole concentration of the conscious mind to be focused on holding the aim and the subsequent loosing.

The actual time involved will vary from one arrow to another since it may take a little longer to settle down on some occasions and this variation in time is a good thing. It puts an elastic area in the time scale from the point of low preparation to loosing and helps to make the decision to loose a conscious one and not a reflex which it never should be.

Loosing the arrow

Press the elbow of the shaft arm back and feel a build-up of pressure against the jaw bone (don't let the string slide away around the *side* of the jaw). Let the shaft hand fingers relax while maintaining the pressure on the jaw by shaft arm movement, and suddenly the arrow will be gone. It may cause a slight surprise when it goes but that is as it should be and makes for an excellent loose.

34. Position before a loose.

Follow-through

The position of full draw should be maintained after the arrow has gone and the eye kept on the target. The purpose of the follow-through is to avoid any deliberate movement of the bow during the time the arrow is being shot from it. During the early part of this action the bow is not only shooting the arrow but is guiding it as well. The speed of the arrow is very high and it is doubtful if the physical re-action of the body to move the bow in any deliberate way could be accomplished in the short time involved to clear the arrow from the bow. However, the principle is a sound one and especially so as it encourages the gaze to be maintained on the target.

35. Position after the loose. Observe how the shaft hand is handing relaxed from the wrist.

At very short ranges like 20 yards (or 20 metres), the arrow will seem to hit the the target at the instant it is loosed, but later on the time it takes to travel the greater ranges will be increased to a second or two and the eye may be tempted to try and follow the arrow. This is a mistake as you can rarely do this. By keeping the follow-through and eye on the target you will see the arrow drop back into view as it lands. You may observe the bow hand jump forward in the direction of the target; this is quite normal and there is no need for concern. The reason for this is that the bow arm is under load when the bowstring is at full draw, but the sudden release of the loose removes this load and your brain is still telling the bow hand to push forward. Reaction times being what they are, your brain cannot tell the arm that the pushing can stop before this involuntary jump takes place. It all happens in the right direction, however, and does not adversely affect the shooting.

Now repeat the process to shoot your other two arrows.

When all three arrows are shot, put the bow back on the ground quiver and leave the shooting position. This is a good time to relax for a moment, for which a camp chair would be very useful; a good time to contemplate the three arrows you have just shot and think over how it was done.

After a couple of minutes rest, place three more arrows in the quiver and take up the standing position once again. Concentrate on doing everything as well as possible and shoot the second three arrows. When this is done hang the bow up and *prepare* to go forward to collect the six arrows shot.

If shooting in company with others remember *not* to go forward to the target until a clear signal that all have shot and are ready to collect, is given.

Collecting the arrows

Do not run down to the target as you could run onto the end of an arrow stuck in the ground and receive a nasty gash on the leg. (You might even damage the arrow!) It is a good idea to walk off the centre line of the target so that any arrows falling short can be seen from an oblique angle and are easily found. It is not very likely that this will be the case at 20 yards (or 20 metres) but it is a good principle to have in mind when the range increases.

Have a good look at the arrows in the target face to see if they have grouped, that is to say, they have landed near each other, or if they are spread about in a random way. If they are grouped, even if not in the middle, you are doing well. If not, then you will need to concentrate a little more on the care with which you shoot the next sets of arrows to achieve as much consistency as possible.

Withdrawing the arrows

Always take care when removing arrows from the target that no-one else is in a position to be jabbed in the face or body by the nock of an arrow. Always make sure that the target is well supported on the stand and take care of your eyes as you withdraw your own arrows when in company with others so as not to injure yourself on another archer's arrows. Never stretch across another person's arrows to reach your own. You may hurt yourself or you may damage the other arrows (and be expected to pay for them on the spot!).

To remove your arrows, place the *back* of the shaft hand against the target face with the fingers opened like a fan with the arrow to be removed in the fork of the first and second fingers. Use the bow hand to take hold of the arrow as near the target face as possible (see Chapter 3, page 50) and pull in a straight line in the direction of the arrow. When the arrow comes out, clamp it under the shaft hand thumb, pile uppermost. Remove all six arrows, tucking each under the thumb and then walk away from the target. If wearing a belt quiver put the arrows away in it.

Some arrows may have missed the target and must be recovered – proceed behind the target keeping a close lookout for the arrows. Those that land on the ground with their fletchings clear can be pulled out in a straight line, rather as if removing them from the target. Others may have their fletchings entangled in the grass. In this case, find the pile end of the arrow first of all and then, holding the pile and gently rotating the arrow, pull it forward and clear of the grass in the direction of travel to avoid damaging the fletchings.

Wet fletchings should preferably be allowed to dry out before they are used again but this is not essential at this stage of shooting.

Return to behind the shooting line, and if in the company of others, make sure *all* are back behind the shooting line and a clear signal is given before shooting is resumed.

If the first set of arrows are not grouped then practice should continue until this begins to happen as discussed earlier. If, however, grouping of the arrows is taking place it is time to correct the aim. For these purposes grouping can be said to be satisfactory if the six arrows in the target could have been contained in a circle 1 foot (30 cm) in diameter or less.

Correcting the aim

To adjust the sight pin on the bow to cause your arrows to land in the centre of the target, proceed as follows: shoot two sets of three arrows (taking care to rest between the two sets of three) with as much care as you can to land the arrows on the target in a group.

Vertical adjustment

Hold the bow out as if at full draw with the sight pin in line with the gold, just as when aiming. Note where the arrows have landed in the target and spot the centre of the group – identify that part of the bow limb above or below the sight pin that corresponds to the group centre and mark it by placing the index finger of the shaft hand on to it, then move the sight pin to that position.

Horizontal adjustment

To correct horizontal sighting *do not* be tempted to move the sight pin in and out – to do so is to compensate for the error, not correct it.

When the body was first positioned on the shooting line this was accomplished by lining up with the centre of the target using the arms raised to shoulder level and the head turned to see and adjust the standing position. This is a good method to begin with but *can* be inaccurate depending on how well you line up the arms with the shoulders. Now that it is possible to use the bow to help, we can establish an accurate body aiming line.

This is done by going through the whole preparation to shoot *without* an arrow, and when the head is turned to the target *both* eyes are closed. Concentrate on feeling right in the full draw position and then open the aiming eye to note where the bow is in relation to the vertical centre line of the target, but *do not move*.

Repeat this about six times and confirm that any variation from the centre is always in the same direction, even if it varies a little. When satisfied on this point, draw up again with the eyes closed. Open the aiming eye, then shuffle the feet a little to rotate the whole body and bow to the correct position. Re-adjust the foot markers and the new position is established. Body aiming should now be corrected. Shoot another six arrows in sets of three to confirm the improved accuracy of the adjustment made.

Shooting for enjoyment

At this stage shooting can continue for half an hour or so just for the pleasure of doing it and to allow a little thought about what has been learned so far.

Breathing and shooting

Breathing and breath control are important in all aspects of physical activity and archery is no exception. In the low preparation position breathing should be relaxed and regular; that is, normal breathing – no special control or rhythm applied to it.

Breathe in as the arms are raised to the high preparation position attempting to inflate the stomach first (you are not, by the way, it is just a feeling) but stop before you experience the feeling of the chest beginning to fill. Breathe steadily out, begin the action of drawing and breathe in at the same time, using the breathing technique as before. When at full draw hold the breath, adjust to the aim from the waist and hold until ready to loose. Keep holding the breath as the pressure of the loose begins and when the arrow shoots, let the breath out in a good steady gush during the follow-through period. Resume normal light breathing.

This method ensures a breath before the drawing of the bow to give a charge of oxygen to the blood. This is followed by a breath again when drawing, giving a further charge of oxygen. The chest cage is not inflated and remains still during aiming and loosing which is, as a result, consistent. *Remember* you are controlling the breathing and it may take a little getting used to at the beginning. The length of time the breath is held will vary depending on how long the hold lasts, but in any case should not be long enough to cause distress.

The control of the breath is a good thing to do and is perfectly safe in fully fit people; however, some may not be so fit or may feel this kind of control is not for them. In that case proceed as before but don't hold the breath, even at full draw, if it is uncomfortable but *do* breathe slowly to inflate and deflate the chest cage progressively when at full draw otherwise, the shoulders may be caused to move, which could have adverse effects on the accuracy of shooting.

Extending the range

The initial distance of 20 yards (or 20 metres) will suffice until the shooting accuracy enables groups to be shot so that all the arrows land in the gold and red positions of the 4 foot (122 cm) diameter target face. When this degree of skill has been achieved move the target a further 10 yards (10 metres) from the shooting line.

Mark the position of the sight pin on the foam strip with a felt pen to identify where the 20 yard mark was in case you wish to use it again. Then, shoot six arrows (in two sets of three) as before with the sight aimed at the gold. The group of arrows should land in the target, but low in relation to the centre. Correct the aim as described earlier and shoot again. The arrows should now be central in the target but the group will probably still be larger. Mark the bow sight foam for 30 yards (30 metres). When the size of the group is all in the gold and red it is time to move back to 40 yards (40 metres).

Observe that the marks on the bow sight track are getting nearer to the arrow shelf – this is normal and is due to the increasing range. Check that each time you aim on these new distances the upper trunk is still being moved as a unit and you are not just raising the bow arm.

This time you may extend to 50 yards (50 metres) range when the arrows are all grouping in the gold, red and blue. Then extend to 60 yards (60 metres) when the same group size has been obtained regularly at this distance.

You are now capable of shooting the traditional short rounds of target archery which use the 60, 50, and 40 yards distances on the 4 foot diameter face and the short metric rounds of 50 and 30 metres on the 80 cm target face.

Shooting faults

The path of progress to this level of skill is not always smooth. Arrows don't always behave as we expect them to and have been known to be wide of the mark or under or over the target. This is a clear indication that some faults are creeping into the shooting technique and in the enthusiasm to shoot you have not maintained concentration. In Chapter 7 there is a summary of common faults which tend to develop and how these can be identified is explained.

The help of an observer

The ideal observer is a properly qualified coach or instructor, but not all beginners have access to these celestial beings! Instead, someone can act as an observer and can give help in a number of valuable ways. Look for the following:

1 *Lining up with the target* Inaccuracy can occur if the arms, when raised level with the shoulders, are not brought back in line with the shoulders or are swinging too far back. An observer standing a yard or two behind the shooting line and in line with the target centre and your standing position, can soon spot this and put you right.

2 *Finding head position using the arrow as a guide* An observer standing as before will see the arrow apparently sticking out of the top of your head. From the observer's point of view, the arrow *should* appear vertical and guidance can be given to make the required corrections if this is not the case. Head position can also be practised at home by using a mirror – you will be able to use your own eye as the target and line up with the arrow and see your relationship. Again, the arrow should appear *vertical* so adjust if it is not. This is an excellent way to practice this important position.

3 *Bow arm position* When the bow is brought up to the horizontal and then turned to the vertical, it may not be vertical and an observer standing as before will see the upper limb above your head and can help to establish this. This is also very true when coming to full draw during early practice because a bow which is tilted from the vertical

when shot can cause a lateral spread of the arrows landing on the target.

4 *Low preparation position* An observer standing a few yards away from you on the shooting line and facing you can see this situation well. Remember – the line through the arrow, through the shaft hand fingers (which should be at right angles to the string), the palm of the shaft hand and wrist and elbow of the shaft arm should all be aligned when you look down at them. From where the observer stands these same parts should also form a straight line from that point of view so the straight line exists in both the vertical and horizontal planes.

5 *High preparation position* When this is achieved you should not try to see this relationship but the observer should see the same straight line simply transferred from the 'low' position and can correct it and help you to feel it correctly.

6 *Drawing the bow* The earlier text stressed the importance of the elbow of the shaft hand being pushed back rather than the bow being pulled. It is often difficult to be sure you are doing this, but an observer can help a great deal. The observer should stand in a convenient position while you adopt the position of full draw *without* actually drawing the bow (rather like being in the follow-through). One hand of the observer should be offered as a hook for the shaft hand fingers to fit into and the other hand placed behind the shaft arm elbow. Pull against the resistance of the fingers, then let the assistant build up pressure of the hand against the elbow and gradually remove the hand securing the shaft hand fingers. What you must do now is deliberately press the elbow against the resistance of the observer's hand and you will probably feel a change of muscles from those inside the upper arm to the ones outside the upper arm and the back muscles will come into play. *That* feeling is the one you should have at the end of drawing the bow.

7 *Getting the loose right* Here are simple exercises that should be practised before shooting begins each time you go to shoot. They can be done at odd times during the day and can make a considerable improvement to the suppleness of the hands and fingers.

Place the palms and fingers of the hands together with the

77

36. Helping to get
    the muscle
    balance correct.

fingers on the right hand matching the fingers on the left hand and the heels of the palms together as close as possible to the wrists (as in prayer perhaps).

Exercise 1 – Extend the elbows sideways to try to form a straight line without letting the heels of the palms separate. This should be done say 50 times at each session until no feeling of tightness exists in the wrist joints. Then you are ready for Exercise 2.

Exercise 2 – Extend the elbows as before and this time separate the heels of the palms *but not the fingers* so as to bend the palms in line (eventually) with the forearms, and effectively bend the fingers back at right angles. This may be rather uncomfortable but keep at it and although you may never make the fully flexed position of the photograph, try to get as close to it as you can.

The next stage in this loosing training is to have the co-operation of the observer as follows: prepare to practise loosing into the ground but when the initial draw has been taken have the observer place a fist on the string and pro-

37. Wrist exercise 1
   – forearms in
   line, heels of
   palms together.

38. Wrist exercise 2
   – fingers bent at
   right angles.

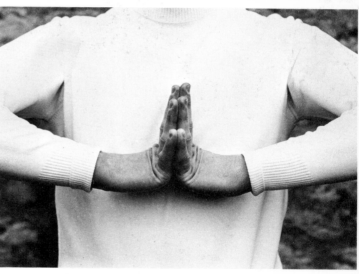

vide the simulated chin resistance normally felt at full draw. Continue the drawing action while the observer keeps the fist resisting until the string escapes from the fingers. Note how the hand jumps back just as it should under the chin.

Blind-loosing – the further stage is to approach the target and measure out a shooting position 5 yards (5 metres) from the target. With the observer standing in line and facing you (as when checking low and high preparation) set up to shoot at the target and when coming onto the aim (a big body movement) close both eyes and CONCEN-

39. Ground loosing with an assistant helps to teach the stringhand how it should react.

TRATE on the action of loosing. Repeat the process for about 15 minutes and check with the observer that the shaft hand is jumping back about an inch and not just staying still or even creeping forward. Have the observer call out when a good one took place and remember what it felt like. Ideally the shaft hand should be totally relaxed and should hang from the wrist after the string escapes.

Important ! The observer must keep an eye on your upper trunk movement and where the arrows land on the target in case you are in danger of shooting over the top.

8 *Checking the full draw position* With the normal shooting distance of 20 yards or more resumed, shoot a few arrows (in sets of three) at the target while the observer adopts the standing position facing you and a few yards away along the shooting line. Ask the observer to use the edge of a book or magazine as a straight edge to check the line when you

are at full draw. The correct line is one that passes from the point on the bow where the bow hand is placed, passes through the second and third fingers of the shaft hand and extends to the elbow of the shaft arm. This is called the Draw Force Line (DFL) and is an important one. When not maintained it causes imbalance in the muscles of the body, leading to early fatigue. It can contribute to faults in technique and, in a bad case, can cause the limbs of the bow to work out of balance which in turn may reduce the life of a bow.

9 *Follow-through* As a final check on the main points, ask the observer to see how well your follow-through position is being maintained after the loose. It *should* be the same as full draw, except the arrow has gone and the bow hand and shaft hand have moved along the DFL to be a little further apart, with the shaft hand tending to hang from the wrist.

10 *Concentration* At various points previous reference has been made to shooting three arrows at an end and not six. The reason for this is that the degree of concentration required to shoot *correctly* is difficult to sustain and experience has shown that any attempt to shoot six arrows straight off results in poorer scores on the later arrows.

5 How to shoot – field archery

This form of archery is practised over rough ground, usually woodland, and preferably undulating. These conditions obviously affect the shooting technique though basic principles remain the same and the degree of application and dedication are as great in field archery as in target.

The fitting of the bracer and finger tab are as before; a quiver of the belt or shoulder-type is desirable since you are much more mobile in this form of archery.

Make sure the arrows to be used are long enough! The arrow length check is similar to target archery except that there should be a minimum of 3 inches beyond the tips of the fingers. This accommodates the longer draw length used in this technique.

Put six arrows in the quiver (but shoot only three at a time). The bow should be braced but sights are not going to be used so the sight pin, if fitted, should be removed. The technique selected in this section is a simple one and the average time to shooting the first arrow is about 10 to 15 minutes.

Training begins on butts of straw bales stacked to about 8 feet high. These are sometimes arranged so that a natural back stop of sloping ground will accept any arrows that miss the target without a long overshoot being involved – in which case a lower butt may be satisfactory. The various shooting distances are usually pegged out to cover the full scope of the distances shot in field archery, which are from 5 yards up to 70 yards on some English and American rounds and 5 metres to 60 metres for the International or FITA field round. This training range should provide a reasonably stable standing position at the shorter distances, say up to 25 yards (25 metres). This allows a more or less natural standing position in the early stages.

Now that the personal equipment is prepared, secure a small target, say 6 inches (15 cm) in diameter, or a suitable aiming mark of similar size on the butt at about chest height.

Take your bow with you to the shooting position. From this point on we will refer to a right-handed person.

Standing position

Adopt a comfortable standing position at a distance of 10 yards (10 metres) from the target with the feet about shoulder width apart and the left shoulder nearest the target. The feet should *both* be behind the distance marker, not standing astride the shooting line as one does in target archery.

Unlike target archery, you will not always be able to choose a conventional standing position. Frequently, one leg may have to be bent at the knee to give a stable line through the shoulders. To achieve this and then aim at the target will often also involve rotation at the waist, so fixing the position of the feet in relation to the shoulders does not apply.

Holding the bow

The hand position on the bow is taken in the same manner as target archery. The same checking method for establishing string clearance is used, and remember, the bow is not to be gripped, just contained in the hand.

Preparation to draw

In the description of these operations in target archery the nocking of the arrow, loosing into the ground etc. were discussed at length and the same principles are followed for field archery. We are then established in the low preparation position, that is: the arrow is on the string, the fingers are in position and light pressure has been applied by pushing the bow away a little to give a positive feel at the finger tips under the tab but the head *has not* been turned to the target.

Positioning the head

This is now achieved by lowering the head to look down at the shaft hand (and see the nock and fingers on the string). Raise the eyes to the horizon and WITHOUT tilting the head, turn to the target with both eyes open. This will produce a vertical head position best suited to the type of anchor point to be used.

Anchor point

Target archers anchor under the chin with the string touching the centre of the jaw and the tip of the nose. The head position is tilted out of the vertical but it results in the aiming eye being positioned vertically above the anchor point. Since the ranges shot in field archery are generally shorter than most of the target archery ranges, the advantage of the higher trajectory, and hence longer range, of the arrow obtained by the under the chin method is not necessary. Aiming without sights is considerably assisted by bringing the arrow closer to eye level when the side face anchor is adopted.

Positioning the bow and establishing an anchor point

Without drawing the bow, simply raise it as if at full draw; that is, with the arm extended fully towards the target but without the elbow joint locked. The shaft hand will, of course, have been released from the string for this checking process and the shaft arm should be raised so that the index finger comes to the corner of the mouth and the forearm is level with the ground. Return to the low preparation position and make ready to draw the bow.

Drawing the bow

This is accomplished in two stages – the first is to raise the bow arm above shoulder level and extend the bow arm pointing towards the target, as before but retaining contact with the shaft hand. (This is the 'Tee' preparation position.) Then, when you are satisfied with the angle of the bow, draw the shaft arm back to establish the index finger tip at the anchor point using the corner of the mouth as your point of reference. This method of drawing involves a lot more shoulder rotation than some other methods that might be used.

Take care each time the draw is made that the shoulders come back into line with the target again. During the latter few inches of the drawing action make sure the shaft arm elbow is being pushed back rather than your hand pulling. This helps to use the correct muscles when the load of full

40. 'Tee' prepara-
tion position.

41. Full draw.

draw should be carried across the back and shoulders.

This method is good in rough country because it positions the bow where it will be before and after shooting and it can be seen to avoid obstructions such as branches of trees which could damage the bow limbs when the bow is shot. Practise this drawing action until confident that you are doing it smoothly, and that you feel comfortable.

Aiming at the target

Fix the gaze on the target centre (both eyes open) and observe in secondary vision where the pile of the arrow seems to be. Keeping the gaze on the centre of the target, move the view of the arrow pile until it relates to the centre of the target. In other words, the pile of the arrow is on a straight line from your eyes to the target.

Remember to move the whole upper body from the waist to come to the aiming position. Don't just move the bow arm. This will shoot the arrows higher than the centre of the target but this can be remedied shortly.

Point of aim sighting method.

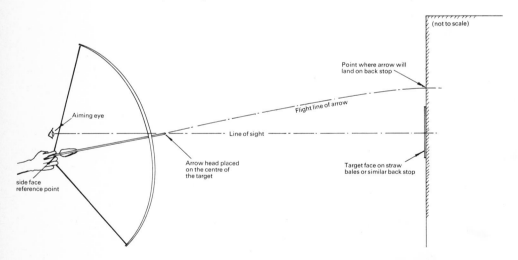

Loosing

When loosing into the ground, the bow string was released by a sudden straightening of the fingers of the shaft hand. This is how the loosing action takes place in this style of shooting. After a holding period to settle down and aim, loose the arrow by deliberately straightening the fingers. Do not be tempted to let the shaft hand creep forward nor try to move it backwards as in target archery.

A good idea is to lightly locate the thumb behind the jaw bone to help stabilize the shaft hand position. Hold the follow-through position of full draw for a few seconds and then come down.

Shoot two more arrows and then retire from the post (shooting position). Return after a couple of minutes and shoot three more arrows. Continue shooting three arrows at a time, in sets of six, recovering the arrows in the same manner as in target archery until groups are established. When this is occurring it indicates that your shooting is becoming consistent and we can take the next step.

Correcting the aim

The method of aiming you have been using is the direct point of aim and the group of arrows were landing rather above the centre of the target. There may also be a lateral deviation, but we will come to that.

The vertical index

Look at the target and relate the *vertical* distance between the centre of the target and the *centre* of the area where the arrows were grouping. If you were to put a mark of some kind below the centre of the target the same distance which your group centre was above it, you could relate the pile of the arrow to it. Aiming on that mark should bring your arrows down and into the target centre. This method would again be the point of aim method.

This method is not convenient in a mobile situation like field archery because you cannot run to the target and put your aiming mark out before you shoot. In fact, the shooting regulations prohibit such things. What you can do is assess the amount below the target by which you should aim and not use a mark at all. This is known as the space picture method. Proceed with this method and correct the aim in the vertical index. It takes a little practice but one soon gets quite good at the assessment required.

You will soon make one observation when shooting at targets on sloping ground. It will be found when shooting uphill the shots will tend to fall lower than expected and when shooting downhill, higher than expected. The change to the space picture to put this right is not a large one but needs to be taken into account, so a good rule to bear in mind is:

steep slope – up: aim up
steep slope – down: aim down

The lateral index

Lateral deviations from the centre are usually a product of either the bow arm's being stiff because of locking of the elbow joint or by a head or eye fault explained in Chapter 7. The elbow fault is easily recognized as it will produce quite a pronounced deviation to the left (for a right-handed archer). Very small corrections are required to produce marked results.

There is another cause of lateral deviation that might occur. This is when the eye over the arrow nock is not sufficiently controlling the aiming. Should other factors seem correct except for pronounced deviation to the left, it is possible that the left eye is having more influence than is desirable. As was explained in target archery, one eye may be dominant. When it is the eye under which the arrow is to be located, all is well, but if it were the other eye it can cause the aim to move too much to the left.

For the sake of simplicity, close or cover the left eye when this problem is suspected and see the effect on your shooting. If the eye is the cause of a left lateral deflection, the closing or covering will produce an immediate correction. When this is proven to be the case you will be obliged to keep the non-aiming eye closed or covered when aiming.

Extending the aim

When you are shooting or grouping well it is time to increase the range. Move back to 15 yards (15 metres) and shoot using the space picture method, estimating how much below the target centre you need to place the arrow pile. There will not be a large difference with only a 5 yard (5 metre) increase in range, but you will probably notice the space picture puts the pile of the arrow a little higher than before.

When ready move back to 20 yards (20 metres) which is the maximum range for the 6 in diameter face. (On the FITA round the maximum range on the 15 cm face is 12 metres.)

The next change of distance should also involve a change of target face to 12 inches in diameter (30 cm) which should be shot at from the 20 yards (20 metres) position. Get used to the change of size and then increase the distance in stages of 5 yards (5 metres) up to 35 yards maximum range for that size of target. (30 metres maximum in FITA rounds at 30 cm diameter targets.) This progression increases with target changes occurring as follows:

Change to 18 in face at 35 yards: use up to 50 yards
    (45 cm face at 30 metres: use up to 45 metres)
Change to 24 in face at 50 yards: use up to 70 yards
    (60 cm face at 45 metres: use up to 60 metres)

By now you are shooting the full range of distances above 10 yards (10 metres) which you will be expected to shoot in field archery, but it pays to become *very good* on the practice butts before attempting to go round the range as a miss may not so much lose you a score as lose you an arrow.

Other methods

The style of Field archery we have discussed in this section is bare bow, which means that no marks are permitted on bow or the string and no aids to aiming may be used as attachments to the bow. The system of aiming is, you will remember, known as space picture method. An alternative form of bare bow is to aim without any deliberate method, but to depend on a snap judgment of the shot at the target. This system is known as instinctive method.

Instinctive method

This method is perhaps the most challenging one to use and brings to mind the relationship that an archer might have with the bow and arrows when having to depend on them to hunt for food. The stalking of the game or the lying in wait could both culminate in a chance to shoot your dinner, which can happen so quickly that there is only time for a snap shot.

The type of shooting we term instinctive depends on the same kind of judgment of distance, height and angles that enables you to screw up a piece of paper and toss it in the waste paper basket. If you *think* about it you would probably miss. This pre-disposition we have to think and make judgments is the very reason why, in instinctive shooting, the first shot is usually the best, at least in those archers who have not yet developed the method properly.

The true instinctive shot is the archer who can shoot each arrow as an event and not be influenced by the result of the previous one. It takes considerable application to close your mind to the event of the last arrow and not be tempted to pre-assess where the next arrow is to go.

The technique sounds simple enough – all you do in shooting is to fix the gaze on the target, usually with both eyes open, bring the bow up and come to full draw quite rapidly and when you feel that you are in the right position, you shoot. This completely ignores any space picture or other kind of conscious assessment. Some archers have a gift for this and seem to do well almost at once – others succeed after years of trying, and in the latter case the author often wonders if they are *unconsciously* using space picture after all!

Free-style
This style uses sights in much the same way as in target archery and distances can be set on the track of the sight in a similar way. The big challenge to the target archer coming to field archery free-style is when shooting a round where distances are not marked.

Field archery can be seen from the foregoing to be a very testing, fascinating sport, worthy of consideration if you are a target archer, as it can be a most exciting and enjoyable alternative. Few, in the opinion of the author, could reach the top in both field and target archery because of the considerable application each of the discipline demands. The fact that some have done so is a credit to their dedication.

6 Care and maintenance of equipment

The value of even a modest programme of care and maintenance will pay handsome dividends in that the useful life of your equipment will be considerably extended. No great skill is required to carry out the tasks outlined in this chapter, and the time can be chosen to suit the archer. The last place to do equipment maintenance is during a tournament or at any time when you are shooting.

The bow

The fibre-glass self-bow, recommended for use in the early stages of archery, is so rugged that very little maintenance is involved. Safety checks should keep you aware of the condition of the bow and, in addition, an occasional check to see that no cracks or splits are developing, is all that is involved.

The composite bow needs a little more attention since it is obviously not as rugged as the training bow: a regular inspection of the bow in general, again looking for splits or cracks in the fibre-glass laminations, in the woodwork, and for any indication of twist developing. These, if found, would call for specialist attention and you should go back to your dealer for advice.

The care of your bow is easy enough – a good coat of wax will preserve it well. When travelling to and from the archery range the bow can be protected by a bowbag, but don't store the bow in that bag. If you have the bad luck to get caught in wet weather, wipe the bow dry before putting it into the bowbag.

No bow should be stored standing on its tip, so hang it up so it is supported horizontally on a pair of supports, preferably at the extremities of the riser.

The bow may be a joy to behold and some archers like to have them hung in their home; a nice idea, but not over the fireplace or over a radiator or other source of direct heat.

Bow strings

The bow, then, seems to look after itself quite well but the bow strings wear out and these are reasonably cheap to buy and easy to obtain. When your bow arrives it will be complete with a string and some details about the string should be recorded for future reference. The length of the string from end to end (including the loops) should be measured. The length inside each loop, the length of the serving at each end of the string, the length and relative position of the centre serving, and the bracing height when fitted on the bow should also be recorded.

With these details it is quite easy to buy a new string and be sure of an accurate duplicate, even if you are unlucky enough to have a break with the only one you have.

A wise archer will have at least two strings in regular use at a time so that both are shot in; that is, fully stretched in use, and dependable. Then, if one were to break the other can be quickly fitted.

Some stretching and settling down will take place in the early stages of use, so the string needs to be 'shot-in' until the bracing height becomes stable. Then, and only then, is it fit to go into your tackle box as a 'spare' to be shot in regular rotation with your other string or strings.

Arrows

The arrows are in many ways the most important part of your tackle and a great deal of pleasure can be gained from shooting arrows which fly true and steady to the mark, knowing that you repaired them yourself.

Fletchings

May be either feathers or plastic vanes and may need attention or to be replaced. They may be liable to damage at the front end if the arrow clips the edge of the boss or perhaps (occasionally) lands in the grass and has to be pulled out pile first.

Replacement sets of feathers, pre-cut to shape and coloured, can be purchased from reputable dealers and it would be worth buying some for stock against future repairs. If, for example, your cock feathers were blue and the flight feathers yellow, you should buy one packet of blue and two packets of yellow to preserve the proportions for three fletched arrows. The packets of feathers *should*, as near as feathers can, exactly match those fitted to your arrows but some checks are needed to make sure. Examine and compare the shape to be satisfied they are the same. Then check that the shiny side and the dull side of the feathers are the same in relation to the shape as those fitted to your arrows. Remember that the shiny side represents the upper surface of the feather and the dull side the lower surface of the feather.

If feathers are all cut from the same side wing of the bird (usually turkey) then they should match in regard to shiny and dull sides. Should feathers have been cut from different wings, i.e. a mixture of left and right wing feathers, they would cause erratic flight of the arrow and be quite useless.

The shaft can be prepared by stripping off the damaged fletchings with a sharp knife. Take care not to dig into the metal of the shafts. Clean the area with a fine grade of emery cloth to remove all the residue and any oxide and 'prime' the surface with a *thin coat* of adhesive spread all over the cleaned area with a finger to seal the surface of the shaft.

Suitable adhesives for feather fletching are Bostick No. 1 and H.M.G. (H. Marcel, Guest), these will also fix plastic vanes and may also be used for nocks and piles. Trade names vary from one country to another but the two mentioned are both available on a world-wide market. Both are waterproof, which is the essential feature. The H.M.G. has a long, thin delivery spout which makes the application very easy.

To place the fletchings correctly on the shaft, a fletching jig will be needed. There are several types on the market and you tend to get what you pay for. The best on the market in the modest price range is the X-AKT fletching jig illustrated. This has a clamp with which to hold the feather or plastic vane being fixed. This fits into place on the frame of the jig and is held in place by a magnet. This allows the clamp to be easily adjusted before final placing. The socket at the base of the jig will accommodate all types of nocks and has an ejection button for the 'keyhole' type. The socket is bushed to rotate and give indexed positions to suit three-fletched and four-fletched arrows. Angular offset can be obtained by adjusting the magnet housing on its slotted base

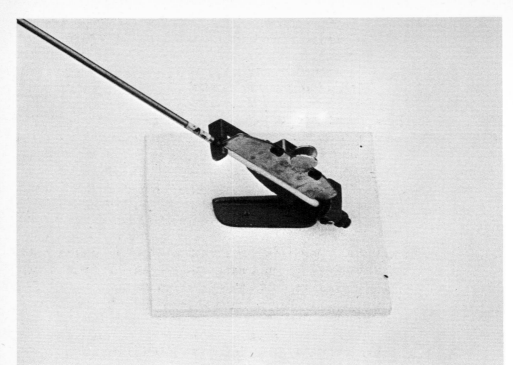

42. The X-AKT
fletching jig
with an arrow
in it.

which enables a fletching to be set at a slight angle to the axis of the arrow shaft.

The fletchings on an arrow are designed to guide it and to make it fly true. To aid this it is desirable that the arrow should rotate in flight and to ensure this happens, the feathers or plastic vanes are usually set on the shaft at an angle of up to $1\frac{1}{2}$ to $2°$. In the case of the feather, the angle of offset should expose the dull side of the feather to the air stream as that side offers the highest resistance to air flow.

Actually, a feather, because one side is smooth and shiny and the other rough and dull, *could* be set on straight and still cause the arrow to rotate due to the aerodynamic effect of the difference between the two surfaces. Some archers prefer this as they feel it is easier to set the feathers in place.

Plastic vanes are made smooth on both sides and *must* be offset, otherwise the arrow will not spin adequately, if at all, to guide the arrow correctly.

So now you have the arrow prepared, the feathers are ready to use, the jig is set up for three fletch and the adhesive is to hand. Using an arrow that has feathers in place, remove the clamp from the jig and place the arrow in the jig frame. Ensure the nock of the arrow is correctly engaged and rotate the socket to bring the cock feather to the top position.

Hold the clamp open and gently place it down over the feather on the arrow, close the clamp over the feather and then mark the clamp with soft pencil to show the position of each end of the base of the feather on the arrow.

Remove the clamp and make the marks more permanent by using an indelible marker. This gives you the position in which to place the new fletchings in the clamp to exactly match the existing ones. Remove the good arrow from the jig and replace it with your stripped and prepared arrow.

Check that the socket has not been moved and select one of the cock feather replacements. Place it in the clamp (make sure it is the correct way round, you don't want to put a fletching on backwards). The ground base of the feather should be firmly placed against the edges of the clamp so that the clamp will support it when pressure is applied.

A continuous thin coat of adhesive should now be applied to the exposed base of the fletching and the clamp placed on the magnet holder with the base of the fletching just clear of the shaft. Gently push the clamp down to the shaft, bringing the base of the fletching into contact to show an even joint throughout its length and leave it to set. After about a quarter of an hour, the clamp can be gently removed leaving the fletching in place on the shaft.

Turn the socket counter-clockwise until a click is heard or felt and the arrow will have rotated 120° to the next fletching position. Using one of the flight feathers, repeat as before placing it on the shaft, and again rotate the base (after removing the clamp) into position for the final feather.

Leave the arrow, preferably overnight, so that the adhesive sets hard, then rasp away the front end of the feather base to give a smooth junction of feather to shaft at that position.

The refletching is now complete. It is not difficult and a little practice will soon show you where safe 'short cuts' can be made. The method described is a reliable one.

The shafts

You will occasionally have the bad luck to bend an arrow, and this will need to be straightened. Many devices are

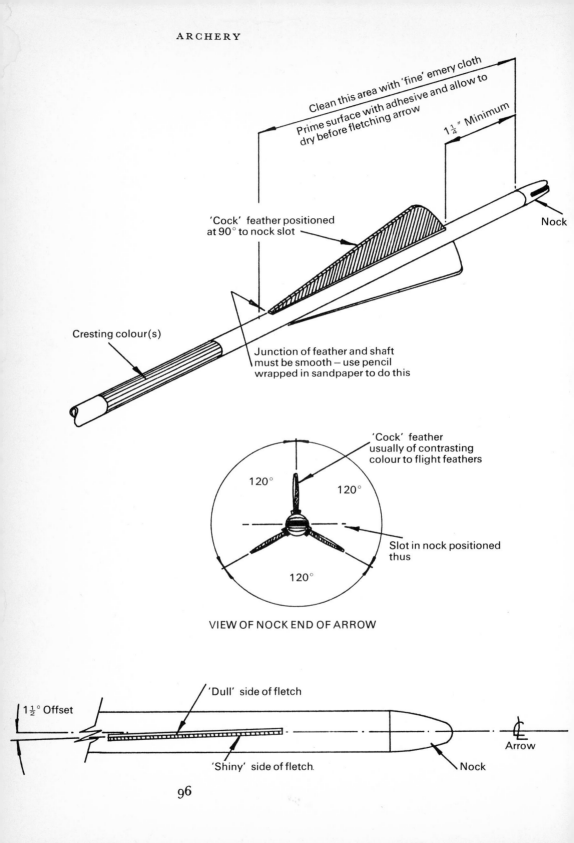

Clean this area with 'fine' emery cloth

Prime surface with adhesive and allow to dry before fletching arrow

$1\frac{1}{4}''$ Minimum

Nock

'Cock' feather positioned at 90° to nock slot

Cresting colour(s)

Junction of feather and shaft must be smooth — use pencil wrapped in sandpaper to do this

'Cock' feather usually of contrasting colour to flight feathers

120°

120°

120°

Slot in nock positioned thus

VIEW OF NOCK END OF ARROW

$1\frac{1}{2}°$ Offset

'Dull' side of fletch

'Shiny' side of fletch.

Nock

Arrow

96

Left Arrow fletching.

Below Ely straightening aid.

Fix nails into wood as shown—cut off nail heads and smooth ends—adjust nail position if required using a new arrow to 'line up' with the edge of the wood.

offered on the market all designed to make this operation easier. They are straightening aids in most cases, and still require a deal of care by the archer in obtaining a straight arrow.

Some dealers provide a straightening service, and if your arrows are of the expensive variety, the dealer is best equipped to do the job. In most cases, however, a reasonable job can be done using a very simple device designed by Guy Ely (see diagram below).

The arrow to be treated is placed in the vees formed by the large screws or nails and the eye is lined up with the edge of the round arrow shaft and the corner edge of the wooden block. Any curve or bend in the arrow can be seen easily and deflected in the opposite direction by thumb pressure until the arrow matches the straight edge of the block.

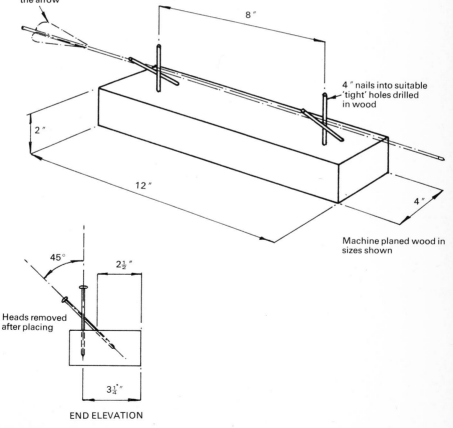

Compare arrow with straight edge of wood (by 'lining up' by eye) and flex with thumbs to straighten, as required, over length of the arrow

8 "

4 " nails into suitable 'tight' holes drilled in wood

2 "

12 "

4 "

Machine planed wood in sizes shown

45°

$2\frac{1}{2}$ "

Heads removed after placing

$3\frac{1}{4}$ "

END ELEVATION

It is a delightful piece of equipment – you make it your-self, and save enough money to be able to buy some really good arrows one day! The whole length of the shaft needs to be checked, of course, and what this aid does is help you to straighten an 8 inch (20 cm) length at a time. The final results are very pleasing and quite badly bent arrows can be restored to a satisfactory condition this way.

Nocks

The nocks of the arrows are quite easy to repair and the old nock, or the remains of it, can be burned off or melted off with a match. The type fitted over a cone-ended tube can be cleaned off with a sharp knife, of course, but the insert type are the ones that need the flame treatment.

When the old nock has been removed, examine the tube end. The cone-end type are not usually damaged, but the open-end tubes may be split. In the latter case, the split shaft has to be cut away and the resulting shortened arrow may suit another archer but is no longer a match for your set. This is the great disadvantage of this type of shaft.

The type of nock fitted over a cone end should be in-spected to see that it is free from faults such as 'burrs' inside the cone. A thin priming coat of adhesive is then applied to the shaft cone and allowed to dry. A small amount of ad-hesive is run into the hollow taper of the nock and the nock fitted over the cone of the shaft. Rotate and spread the wet adhesive, line up the slot in the nock to be at 90° to the cock feather (if there is one) and leave to dry.

The inserted nocks come in two basic types, plain 'spigot-ted' and 'threaded'. The first type fit into a tube which is smooth inside whilst the other type is used in tubes having an internal thread.

The smooth type needs only to be coated with a thin layer of adhesive and pushed into place, rotated and positioned in relation to the fletchings and then the job is done. The threaded type should be screwed into place using a proper nock key which looks like a key from a grandfather clock, is tubular and has a bar inside to engage the slot of the nock. These arrows are, in fact, going out of popularity and the reader may never be involved with them.

Piles

Pile ends of arrows should be kept sharp and well shaped.

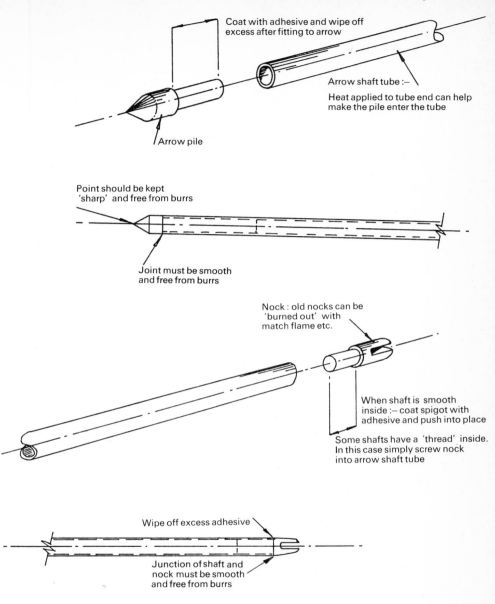

Coat with adhesive and wipe off
excess after fitting to arrow

Arrow shaft tube :—

Heat applied to tube end can help
make the pile enter the tube

Arrow pile

Point should be kept
'sharp' and free from burrs

Joint must be smooth
and free from burrs

Nock : old nocks can be
'burned out' with
match flame etc.

When shaft is smooth
inside :— coat spigot with
adhesive and push into place

Some shafts have a 'thread' inside.
In this case simply screw nock
into arrow shaft tube

Wipe off excess adhesive

Junction of shaft and
nock must be smooth
and free from burrs

Arrow piles and
nocks.

Note
If fletchings are on
arrow when fitting
new nock ensure
nock is positioned
with string slot at
90° to cock feather.

Most of them are steel and a small file will do a good job in helping to keep them in good order. Replacement of piles is not difficult but any pile replacing an old one must be the same weight or the matching of the arrow will be adversely affected.

99

A pile can be removed by gently heating the pile and tube in hot water. Aluminium expands at about twice the rate of steel and the tube will expand away from the spigot of the pile. A pair of pliers applied to the pile and *gentle* rotation and pulling will usually release it. Never put the arrows on an electrical hotplate or into the flame of a gas burner to heat the ends up. This could have disastrous effects on the heat treatment given to the aluminium tubes and ruin them completely.

The new pile should be compared with the old one and the spigot length cut down as necessary to make as good a match with the old one as possible. Coat the spigot with adhesive and insert into the tube after warming the tube again. Leave to set after wiping off any excess adhesive.

All of these maintenance jobs are great fun to do and can occupy an evening when, perhaps due to weather, or other circumstances, you are not able to go out shooting. Some archers become so fascinated by this side of the sport that they become suppliers to all their club friends. Some graduate to bow making, others to making associated leather goods. There is simply no limit to archery and all its varied interests.

7 Correcting faults

The next phase of normal development that we can expect to take place will be that your shooting will improve with continued practice, but may be impaired by the unconscious development of some faults in your shooting technique. How can we recognise and deal with shooting faults? Ideally one should go to a qualified coach who has the skill needed to analyse what is happening and lay out a programme of corrective training. This is not always possible, unfortunately, so other means of sorting out shooting faults will be necessary.

Can we analyse our own shooting? Up to a point, yes, but it has its limitations. In Chapter 4 the learning process was mentioned: the brain records patterns of activity and recognizes a duplication or series of duplications. A distinct set of reflexes then develops, the body and brain are in harmony and feel right when carrying out the activity.

This all works well when we learn to do things correctly, but small and apparently insignificant variations from the ideal technique can occur and go unnoticed long enough to be repeated and become a reflex pattern. This is not always a bad thing. The body may adapt to the technique and an individual style develop, which no good coach would seek to inhibit. However, factors in our shooting can develop which do not help to give good results and lead to further deterioration and the introduction of variables. It has been said earlier that a technique that is consistent is generally a good technique and from that it follows that a shooting technique containing variables must be a bad one. Since our shooting has developed we probably feel right in what we are doing, so self-analysis becomes difficult, even impossible, for anything other than the most glaring errors. We need some help, then, to do the job properly and we can call upon the services of an assistant who can look at what you are *actually* doing. Provided some understanding exists about where, and how, to look, even an untrained observer can be very helpful.

Keys to analysis

Coaches, during their training, are given three basic keys to analysis for use when studying an archer. They apply just as much to field archers as they do to target archers.

1 Preparation line (prep. line): an imaginary line that runs from the elbow of the shaft arm through the loosing fingers on the bow string, along the arrow to the bow. It is seen at waist level *before* the archer begins to draw the bow.

2 Draw force line (DFL): an imaginary line that runs from the point of pressure on the bow handle, through the nock of the arrow, to the point of the shaft arm elbow when the archer is at full draw.

3 Eye, sight, arrow relationship (ESAR): this relationship is correct when the centre of the aiming eye is *vertically* above the anchor point (or reference point) on the chin or face and the pin of the sight is *vertically* above the pile of the arrow when the bow is at full draw. The relationship is concerned with the tilt of the head and any cant or tilting of the bow that might *unintentionally* take place.

There are other factors in the shooting technique that can go wrong and these will be included, but if the basic technique is correctly observed and associated with the three keys to analysis described above, a good basis for the study of an archer to seek and identify shooting faults exists.

Equipment

The tackle can be a source of variables and needs to be eliminated as a cause of problems before any analysis of the shooting begins, so examine it to ensure that the following points are correct:

The bow

1 The bracing height should be correct at the setting you normally use.

2 The nocking point should be clear and firmly in place. A nocking point that moves would cause vertical errors. See

that it is set at the usual amount above the arrow shelf.

3 The arrow rest, if one is fitted, should be in good condition. Some types have a small leaf spring or finger to support the arrow, which should not be damaged.

4 The sight track must be secure on the bow and any sight pin made to adjust up and down must be clamped firmly so as not to move when the bow is shot.

5 The sight pin should be set so that the centre of the pin head is projecting no more than half the diameter of the arrow shaft. ($\frac{1}{4}$ in diameter arrow, means a $\frac{1}{8}$ in projection of pin.)

The arrows
1 Spin all the arrows to be sure they are straight.

2 See that all the nocks are a good fit on the nocking point and all feel the same degree of resistance when engaged on the string; that is, no tight or loose nocks among them.

3 See that the fletchings are in good condition and that they are *all* from the same side wing of the bird.

The finger tab
1 This should be a good fit without an excess of material beyond the finger tips or the top edge of the index finger.

2 The surface should be smooth. A hair tab must not be worn to the point of baldness in places.

The bracer
1 This should be a good fit.

When these points have been checked then it would be reasonable to expect any variable results in shooting accuracy to be due to your shooting and not the fault of the equipment.

Shooting
The archer should now begin shooting at a moderate range

and shoot with all arrows aimed at the centre *without* regard to where the arrows are actually landing on the target face. No adjustment or aiming off should be made at this time.

The observer should look at all the stages of preparation from the time of setting up the initial standing position to the subsequent loose and follow-through. Compare the archer's actions and positions with the correct ones explained or illustrated in this book and record, in a note pad preferably, those that differ.

This could easily take an hour or so to do, but don't spoil it by making hasty conclusions – the notes on the pad are *differences* from basic technique but may *not* be faults, so the next stage is to look at each of the differences you have observed and decide if the difference is a variable action or done in a consistent manner. Mark those that are consistent and they can be put aside for the moment as it is the variable factors that will need attention first. This might sound a bit difficult, but it is not, and at this stage the sort of things we would be expecting to find are obvious variables. Here are a few examples to look for:

Standing position
1 Failing to line up the body with the target.

2 Failing to use foot markers to maintain consistency. Not checking each time that the toes are properly related to the foot markers. (Not applicable to field archers.)

Bow-hand position
1 The bow-hand thumb pad should carry the pressure of the bow – some people tend to turn the hand into the bow too far and this will cause the bow string to jerk side-ways away from the bow arm, and can be clearly seen at the moment the arrow is loosed. It should not be confused with a gentle swing of the bow and string, away from the bow arm, which is acceptable; the fault will be a pronounced jerk.

2 The bow hand can be dropped or heeled so that the pressure of the full width of the little finger side of the bow hand is applied to the handle – this can be confirmed if the bottom limb of the bow is seen to jerk forward at the moment the arrow is shot. Again, a gentle swing is acceptable, but not a pronounced jerk.

Bow-arm elbow

This should not be locked, and if allowed to be extended to the locked position a side-ways jerk of the bow will be seen when the arrow is shot. A gentle swing, once again, is acceptable but no jerk.

Bow-arm shoulder

This should be relaxed and in line with the shaft-arm shoulder so that a line projected forward would intersect the target. If the shoulder is turned or rolled in towards the line of the arrow at full draw, this will be seen to project a line through the shoulders that will pass outside the target width and the effect on the bow will be similar to a stiff elbow.

Head position

1 The head position *must* be consistent if good results are to be attained and *must* be tilted the correct amount. Have the *arrow held to nose and chin* check carried out by the archer from time to time and stand behind him in line with the target. The arrow should seem to stick vertically out of the top of his head. Incorrect tilting will cause arrows to spread across the target as they are shot, e.g. for a right-handed archer too much tilt will put the arrows to the left of centre – not enough tilt will put arrows to the right of centre.

2 The front centre of the *chin* and the tip of the *nose* should be touching the string. Lack of contact with the nose will cause vertical errors on the target face (target archery only).

The string hand

1 Fingers should be applied to the string at right angles, with the load being carried by the second and third fingers – a small gap between the arrow and second finger is important.

2 The finger tips should be crooked to retain the bow string but the second joints should not be bent to make the fingers into claws as this may lead to a bad loose.

3 The top finger should touch the underside of the chin at full draw (target archery) and no gap should occur. A gap occurring is a variable factor which will cause a vertical error on the target.

4 The string hand should not drag the string around to either side of the centre of the jaw or the arrow will go off centre in the horizontal plane on the target face.

5 The field archer comes to a reference point on the side of the face which could be marked for the purposes of these assessments to ensure that the position is consistently maintained.

6 The target archer's loose should result in a clean jump of the hand backwards from the chin. There should be no creeping of the string away from the chin before it is released from the fingers.

7 The field archer's loose is accomplished by a swift straightening of the fingers and the hand should not move other than that. No creeping of the string should be observed.

8 The fingers of the string hand should come off the string together, never 3,2,1 or 1,2,3.

9 The string fingers and hand should never jump away sideways from the chin or face at the moment of loose.

The shaft-arm elbow
Should always lie on the DFL and can be checked by lining up the edge of a note pad or book with the bow hand and arrow nock when the observer stands some distance away. A fault seen here will often be due to incorrect application of the fingers to the string rather than a direct fault in itself; it will lead to vertical errors on the target face.

The bow
The archer should hold the bow vertically and not cant it in either direction, as seen from behind the archer. If the bow is canted it will cause horizontal errors on the target face.

The draw length
This needs to be maintained from the time full draw is achieved until its loose has occurred. This is easily seen by observing (from a safe position, of course) that the arrow pile does not slide backwards and forwards on the arrow shelf during the time between full draw and loosing.

Unit aiming

The movement of the archer, from the waist, when coming to the aim should be observed – raising and lowering the bow arm will not do. A fault would cause vertical errors on the target face.

Holding

The period after full draw and taking aim which allows for a settling down period – this may vary in time without any cause for concern, but *must exist* – it prevents the archer loosing off at the target while still on the move and coming to aim, or at least, is intended to do so.

Follow-through

The maintenance of the body position which existed before the loose took place after the loose, with the exception that the bow hand and string hand will probably have moved a little further apart along the DFL. A dramatic change of position after the loose may well indicate a fault in the DFL.

Target face

The next aid to analysis that can be employed is to note the pattern of error on the target face and see what we can learn from it. Generally, the arrows will tend to group on the target if the shooting of the archer being observed is reasonable. Very bad shooting containing several variables can cause a scatter of arrows all over the target face and renders this aid to analysis useless.

Target face divided into quarters for fault finding.

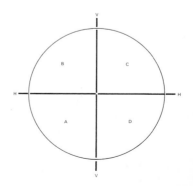

The above diagram shows the target face divided by a vertical line V-V and a horizontal line H-H into four quarters marked A, B, C, and D (starting bottom left).

The following list helps to identify causes in shooting technique which will land arrows in the specified areas, or in the lines, of the target which can then be checked out by a closer study of what the archer is doing.

Arrows landing on or near line V-V above the centre
1 Gap between chin and top finger of string hand (target archers)
2 Lowering of hand on side of face relative to reference point (field archers)
3 Gap between the teeth or the mouth open at time of loose (target archers)
4 Fingers coming off the bow string 3-2-1
5 Heeling the bow handle

Arrows landing on or near line V-V below the centre
1 Nose not in contact with the string, allowing head to tilt back (target archer)
2 Raising hand on side of face relative to reference point (field archer)
3 Shooting with a high elbow on the shaft arm, causing the bow to drop after the loose
4 Fingers leaving the bow string 1-2-3 instead of together at at the same time.

Arrows landing on or near line H-H to left of centre (right-handed archers)
1 The non-aiming eye having too much influence on the aim
2 Bow-arm elbow locked instead of slightly bent
3 Bow canted so that the top limb has moved to the right
4 Bow hand into the bow too far causing it to jerk the string away from the bow arm
5 Head not turned far enough

Arrows landing on or near line H-H to the right of centre (right-handed archers)
1 Bow canted so that the top limb has moved to the left
2 Head turned too far
3 Arrow anchored on the left of chin centre line

Arrows landing in the zone marked A (right-handed archers)

1 Creeping: the string being permitted to creep away from the anchor point (or reference point) before being released from the fingers
2 Forward loosing: the string hand moving forward instead of backwards at the moment of loosing (a field archer should *not* move the hand back but could forward loose)
3 Bow arm not extended correctly causing the arrows to be under-drawn
4 String clearance inadequate, causing the bow string to drag on the bracer

Arrows landing in the zone marked B (right-handed archers)

1 String hand sliding to the right of the anchor point before the loose takes place, thus displacing the nock of the arrow to the right and increasing the draw length
2 The bow arm being pushed out to a locked elbow just before the loose leading to an increase in draw length combined with the sideways jerk of the bow arm due to the locked elbow
3 Bow hand turned into the bow too far, combined with heeling the bow handle

Arrows landing in the zone marked C (right-handed archers)

An overdrawn arrow will go here provided that the over-draw is a simple error and not combined with other errors, with the possible exception of canting the top of the bow to the left.

Arrows landing in the zone marked D (right-handed archers)

Arrows that land in this area of the target would land there as part of a general scatter on the target and would not group in that position, so for our purposes, this zone of the target has little to tell us.

General observations

The nature of the pattern of errors, if studied closely, will soon reveal that the kind of faults that impair the mechanical efficiency of the bow will usually put arrows low on the target. Those that artificially increase the amount of force applied to an arrow (such as overdrawing) will usually put arrows high on the target.

Any fault that causes the bow to displace from the balanced position by a sudden jerk will usually displace the arrow in the direction the bow finishes pointing in. For example, a bow that is heeled will usually finish pointing high in relation to the DFL and the arrow will tend to go high.

The term 'pointing the bow' is taken to be an imaginary line from the nocking point, across the arrow shelf and extended forward beyond the bow and represents the relative position of the arrow as it is shot *just before* it leaves the bow string.

Corrective training

When all the variables, that is, inconsistent factors of the shooting technique, have been determined, the next step is to tackle the faults systematically.

The best way to tackle the inconsistent factors is to treat them in the order in which they take place in the explanations of shooting technique given in Chapters 4 and 5. Each fault should be tackled in isolation as far as possible, and the others totally ignored while this is going on. Some will probably disappear of their own accord if they are actually secondary inconsistencies developing from a major one occurring earlier in the sequence. Remember the learning process; you have to repeat, and repeat, and repeat until the new experience feels right and becomes an integral part of what you are doing under the direction of the subconscious mind.

This gradual process of retraining or correction is good because each part can be learned well, and this is vital. If the corrective training is not carried on long enough, and the new method has not overlaid the old way sufficiently well, there is the strong possibility that under conditions of stress or pressure, such as at a tournament, the old method may break through the trained or conditioned responses and influence the shooting again.

8 Competition in tournament

As your skill grows and develops, the spirit of competition will probably grow too and this is how it should be. Take care to attend practice sessions as opposed to shooting for scores and see also that the social side of your club life is not neglected. The activities of your archery club should bring you to meet and compete with other clubs either in club competitions or in tournaments.

Tournaments

The first time you attend a tournament will be an experience you are likely to remember for a very long time, so you might as well start with thorough preparation and a clear plan of campaign.

Make sure the tackle you are taking is in the best condition it is possible for you to achieve, and that should include all tackle, including spare strings (properly shot in), wet weather gear, the all-important chair and any other items that help you to feel comfortable in the shooting situation.

The route to the tournament ground should be written out in a clear, concise manner which is easy to follow at a glance, so eyes are not going to be taken off the road if you are driving alone – better still, travel with others.

Always leave early enough to allow for a few minor delays (a punctured tyre, for example) and to arrive at the shooting ground a good hour or so before the tournament begins. The organizers need to know that you have arrived, so check in as soon as you can. The target allocated to you will be given at the check-in or registration point and you should move your tackle there and carry out your necessary preparations in a *methodical and leisurely manner* – nothing should be rushed.

With your preparations made, you should now have time to soak up the scenery and get used to your surroundings. The shooting grounds are often set in beautiful country which you would never have seen had you not gone there to shoot. So enjoy them and spend a little time strolling around and breathing good lungfuls of fresh air.

This all helps your preparation. When shooting begins you will probably find yourself a little tense; this is perfectly natural and is due to the effects of certain glands in the body which prepare and arouse the body for what is to come. The outcome will be a feeling of butterflies in the tummy and speeding-up of the heart rate. This is a normal physical effect and is not nerves or anxiety or any other of those things and should not be looked on as something that sets you apart from others or makes you any less equipped to succeed than others are.

This feeling passes off gradually and the heart rate will also drop, but during the first dozen arrows, possibly two dozen at first, it would be a good policy to do a little deep breathing when sitting on your chair between ends of arrows. This sitting and breathing should be carried out in a very deliberate manner, as follows: sit in the chair, back as straight as possible and well supported by the chair back. The angle of the knee joint should be not much more than 90° so that the legs are well supported by the feet which should be either vertically under the knees or further forward. With chairs that have arm rests, the arms may rest on these provided this does not cause the shoulders to lift, otherwise, do as you would do with a chair that does not have arm rests – let the arms hang with the *back* of the wrist resting on the thigh muscles and the palms upwards, fingers relaxed. (This is how boxers sit between rounds, and for the very good reason that it is a very relaxing position – try it.)

The breathing should be deep and when breathing in, seek to inflate the tummy first and then the lungs to full capacity, hold a couple of seconds and exhale in a steady stream until all the air is pushed out. Repeat this about six times and then resume normal breathing rate and all the time remain relaxed in your chair without slumping.

These preparations will make you able to perform to your best level, but do yourself the favour of recognizing your state of progress and don't expect to shoot significantly better than that at the tournament – but you should not be satisfied to shoot a poorer standard either.

Treat each arrow as an event, it is quite useless to worry about a bad arrow you have just shot. It can't be shot again so FORGET IT and focus your mind on shooting the next arrow properly. As the tournament progresses you will probably have a meal break to fit in – don't be tempted to eat a lot, a small meal of cheese and fresh fruit together with an energy giving drink such as 'Dynamo' or similar glucose loaded drink will do more good than a steak and chips or a load of sandwiches. If you can avoid drinking a large volume then do so. You will need to replace losses due to perspiration, but any more than that is not essential – bladder discomfort will be avoided and the moderate meal will not put heavy demands on the digestion, thus the blood oxygen is better used to drive your brain and muscles.

At the end of the day be content with your results at this your first tournament. Analyse what happened during the day and if you did less well than you had hoped, see if you can eliminate the cause in future practice.

Later you will eliminate the cause in practice. Eventually you will come to realize that the strong foundation blocks upon which you have built your technique will not in themselves be enough to take you to the top.

There will come a time when more knowledge will be needed to select the sophisticated equipment and develop advanced techniques which may be obtained from direct personal coaching by coaches of high standard and wide experience.

Most countries have coaching schemes, and if in doubt about the best coaches to go to, contact the appropriate national governing body and through them, the National Coaching Officer who can give you direct advice on the coaches you can approach.

Always keep in mind that you go out to shoot to enjoy your archery and the social contact and exercise that goes with it. You are now a fully competitive archer and will continue to grow and develop in the wonderful sport of archery which will take you to many places that you might never otherwise have seen, lead you to meet interesting people you might otherwise not have met and give you, the writer hopes, an abiding interest to follow all the rest of your life. Welcome archer, you have *started*.

Appendix 1: Glossary of terms

Anchor point Fixed position on the archer's face, or chin, to which the nock of the arrow is drawn.

Arrow pass Part of the side of a bow against which the arrow lies.

Arrow rest A device above the bow handle on which the arrow rests during the draw.

Arrow shelf A part of the handle on a beginner's bow used as an arrow rest.

Back The surface of the bow furthest from the string.

Bare bow The act of shooting without sights. It usually applies to Field archery.

Blunt The type of arrow fitted with a large diameter head with a flat face striking the target instead of a point – used often in hunting birds and small game.

Bolt The name given to the type of arrow used with a cross-bow and not discussed in this book.

Bouncer An arrow that hits the target but fails to penetrate and bounces off to fall to the ground.

Bow sight A device fitted to a bow as an aid to aiming.

Brace The act of fitting the string to a bow in preparation for shooting.

Bracer Device worn on the bow arm to keep clothing out of the path of the bow string.

Bracing height The distance between the bow string and a defined checking point on the bow.

Boss A circular target-backing made of straw, or other material, upon which the target is fixed. Designed to be mounted on a target stand.

Butt A permanent structure of earth or straw bales.

Cast A term applied to the power of a bow to project an arrow, i.e. good cast, fast cast, poor cast etc.

Clout An old English word for a patch or piece of cloth which would be used to mark the target in Clout shooting and may have been arranged as a flag or simply dropped on the ground.

Cock feather The fletching at right angles to the arrow nock.

Composite A bow which has a composition of materials bonded together to form the limbs.

Creep Failure to maintain the draw length while on 'hold'.

Cresting The colour bands on the arrow.

DFL 'Draw force line'. An imaginary line which should be a straight line between the point of pressure on the bow handle, the middle finger of the shaft hand and the point of the elbow of the shaft arm when at full draw.

Dead loose A loose in which only the fingers move to release the bow string.

Dowel A round rod from which wooden arrows are made. (Not recommended – see Chapter 2.)

Draw length 1 The distance to which an archer is capable of drawing efficiently.

2 The distance to which the bow is designed to be drawn.

Draw weight The force required to draw the bow a stated distance, e.g. 36 lbs at 26 inches.

End Three or six arrows shot before collection.

Face	1 The surface of the bow nearest to the bow string. 2 The paper (or other material) target secured to the boss or butt.
Fast	The warning cry meaning 'do not shoot', or 'come down' if the bow is raised. Usually an emergency situation.
Flight feathers	The fletchings that lie nearest the bow opposite the cock feather.
Fletchings	The feathers or vanes on an arrow.
Field captain	The person in charge of shooting when a number of archers are shooting together.
FITA	Federation Internationale de Tir à l'Arc, the governing body of world amateur archery.
Follow-through	The maintenance of the position of full draw after the loose *except* the hands have moved a little further apart and the shaft hand hangs, relaxed, from the wrist.
Forward loose	A loose in which the shaft hand leaves the anchor point and moves forward before the bow string escapes.
Free style	A form of Field archery in which sights are permitted.
Gold	The highest scoring zone in the centre of the target.
GNAS	Grand National Archery Society.
Ground quiver	A holder for arrows (and bow) fixed in or standing on the ground.
Grouping	Shooting arrows close together on the target.
Handle	The part of a bow contained in the hand.
Heeling	Pressing on the bow handle with the heel of the hand, causing the lower limb to bend more than the upper limb.
Holding	The time between establishing the aim and taking the decision to shoot.

Instinctive shooting	The form of Field archery when no sights are used and no deliberate aiming is carried out by the archer.
Lateral index	The imaginary line drawn horizontally through the centre of the target – used in analysis of errors in shooting.
Limb	The *working* part of the bow above or below the handle.
Loose	The moment the bow string escapes from the shaft hand fingers after the decision to shoot has been taken. May also be called the release.
Mark	The object which the archer intends to hit.
NAA	National Archery Association of the United States.
Nock	1 The slot at the end of the arrow which fits on the bow string. 2 The notches on the bow limbs which accept the loops of the bow string.
Nocking point	An indication on the bow string identifying where the arrow nock should be fitted.
Over-bowed	Using a bow that is too strong to be managed efficiently.
Over-drawing	1 Drawing the arrow clear of the arrow pass. 2 Drawing the bow further than its recommended limit.
Pair	A traditional set of three arrows, being two (a pair) and one spare arrow.
Perfect end	A set of arrows which have all hit the centre and thus made a maximum score.
Pile	The pointed end of the arrow.
Point of aim	Aiming by means of referring the pile of the arrow to some aiming point, not necessarily the target.
Post	A place from which to shoot in Field archery indicated by a wooden stake or similar.

Prep-line — The desirable straight line before drawing which passes through the arrow and fore-arm of the shaft-arm, when seen by the archer looking down.

Quiver — A holder for arrows, either carried on the person or fixed (see ground quiver).

Release — The common expression used in the United States meaning the same as loose.

Riser — The *non-working* part of the bow above and below the handle to which the limbs are attached.

Round — A given number of arrows shot under specified conditions.

Self bow — A bow made from one piece of material.

Serving — The whipping on the string to reduce wear from the shaft hand fingers.

Shaft — The section of an arrow between the pile and the nock.

Shooting line — The line across which the target archer stands when shooting.

Sighters — Unscored arrows allowed to be shot before a round so that sights may be checked.

Sling — A device to enable the bow to be shot with an 'open' bow hand.

Snap shooting — Loosing without pause or aim.

Spine rating — The measure of the flexibility of an arrow.

Tab — A shaped piece of leather or similar material worn on the shaft hand fingers to provide a consistent surface for the bow string.

Target — A paper or fabric cover with the scoring zones marked on it, designed to be secured to a target boss or butt.

Underbowed — Using a weaker bow than is desirable.

Unbrace	The act of removing a bow string from the braced position.
Underbraced	A bow in which the bracing height is lower than required – possibly caused by a pending failure of the bow string.
Vane	The plastic equivalent of a feather fletching.
Vertical index	The imaginary line drawn vertically through the centre of the target, used in analysis of errors in shooting.

Appendix 2: List of English-speaking archery societies

Archery Association of Australia

Mr F. Gavin,
22 London Drive,
West Wollongong 2500,
New South Wales,
Australia

Federation of Canadian Archers

Mr Fred Usher,
2677 Dunlevy Street,
Victoria, B.C.,
Canada

Irish National Archery Federation

Mr J. Conroy,
103 St Brendans Avenue,
Malahide Road,
Dublin 5,
Ireland

Grand National Archery Society

Mr J.J. Bray
The Secretary,
Grand National Archery Society,
N.A.C.,
Stonleigh,
Kenilworth,
Warwicks

Archery Association of India

Mr G.N. Mehra,
23 Darya Ganj,
Delhi 6,
India

The Israel Amateur Archery Association

Mr Gershon Huberman,
P.O. Box 286,
Ramat,
Gan,
Israel

The Royal Archery Association of Jordan

Mr D.H. Ledger,
P.O. Box 920,
Amman,
Jordan

New Zealand Archery Association

Mr C. Hoddinott,
37 Tennyson Avenue,
Lower Hutt,
New Zealand

Archery Association of Singapore

Mr Steven Tan Kia Heng,
93B Prince Charles Crescent,
Block 69,
Singapore 3

Rhodesian Archery Association

Mrs M. Potter,
4 Posselt Road,
North End,
Bulawayo,
Rhodesia

South African National Archery Association

Mr J. Everson,
58 Umgeni Road,
Farrarmere,
Benoni 1500,
Transvaal,
South Africa

National Archery Association of the United States

Mr C. B. Shenk,
1961 Geraldson Drive,
Lancaster,
Pennsylvania 17601,
U.S.A.